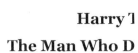

Harry T
The Man Who D

By Jack Steinberg

©Copyright 2016 WE CANT BE BEAT LLC

Copyright 2016 by Jack Steinberg.

Published by WE CANT BE BEAT LLC

Krob817@yahoo.com

Table of Contents

Prologue 5

Chapter 1 8

Early Life 8

Chapter 2 18

World War I 18

Chapter 3 36

Introduction to Politics................................36

Chapter 4 53

Vice President 53

Chapter 5 62

The President Who Dropped the Bomb 62

Chapter 6 75

The United States and the Postwar World 75

Chapter 7...90

The Iron Curtain and the Truman Doctrine 90

Chapter 8 141

United Nations, NATO, and the Warsaw Pact 141

Chapter 9 149

Harry Truman and the Korean War 149

Chapter 10 181

Legacy on American Politics...................................181

Epilogue 205

Bibliography 212

Prologue

When asked about America's presidents, most Americans will readily point out several key individuals: Washington, Lincoln, the Roosevelts, Kennedy, and Reagan. These individuals all stand out because of the trying times in which they served. They were there when our country was created, and they were there when our country was tearing itself apart. They were there when we took on Big Business, and when the world had reached its darkest hour. They are remembered for the tragic shortness of their lives, and for bringing an end to the most uncertain period in world history. These men are remembered for the way they handled these events, and for being the right person at the right time. Their actions and resolve during times of turmoil make them easy candidates for the annals of posterity.

Unfortunately for others, their presidency was not highlighted by momentous occasions.

They were elected, they assumed their office, and they departed with little fanfare. Others came onto the stage and were overshadowed by their successors. Despite the several contributions they themselves made, their names do not come as easily to the American mind as those giants mentioned previously.

Chief among these forgotten leaders is Harry Truman, who had the misfortune of becoming America's 33rd president following the death of Franklin Delano Roosevelt. No other president has redefined the role of the American government in the lives of the people as much as Franklin Roosevelt. No other president was elected to four terms in office. No other president managed to steer America through the grips of a Great Depression and then immediately through the deadliest war in human history. Coming almost as a footnote at the end of the life of this great leader, Harry Truman assumed the reins of government as everything was coming to a close. When Americans think back to World War II, they think Roosevelt.

When Americans think back to the Cold War, they think of Eisenhower or Kennedy. Forgotten is the man who grabbed the helm when the waters became toughest. Forgotten is the man responsible for the end of the Second World War, and the man responsible for the Cold War. For most, Harry Truman appears as a blip on the radar of American history, and his role in our nation's history is overshadowed by those who became before and after him.

Chapter 1

Early Life

You know that being an American is more than a matter of where your parents came from. It is a belief that all men are created free and equal and that everyone deserves an even break.

\- Harry Truman

Harry Truman stood behind Franklin Roosevelt as the President was sworn into office for the fourth time. He looked out over the faces of the assembled crowd. Despite the long years of war, despite the still lingering feeling of the Great Depression, the audience seemed exhilarated. Maybe they could sense that the end of the war was in sight, or maybe they were happy to have the day off of work. As Harry glanced out at them, he figured it probably had more to do with the captivating individual standing at the podium. He knew about the braces that kept the President standing; he thought it was a fitting metaphor, as the President had done so much to brace the American people through so many trials and tribulations.

He stood there grinning as the President issued his fourth inaugural address. No other President in American history had served for so long; perhaps no other President could have counted on the people's continued faith after twelve years in office. But Harry wasn't grinning for that breach of precedent. Harry was grinning because, for some unknown reason, the President had selected him to join the ticket. As Franklin Delano Roosevelt was being sworn into office, Harry S. Truman was becoming the nation's second-in-command, the nation's Vice President. He couldn't help but smile, even though he knew just how burdensome the job could be. For a farm boy from the "Show Me" state, Truman had demonstrated just how achievable the American Dream was.

In 1884, Harry Truman was born in Lamar, Missouri, to John and Martha Truman. He was the firstborn of their three children; they later had another boy, John Vivian, and a girl, Mary Jane. The Trumans were a family struggling to make it in America's vast plains, their respective families having moved westward during the period of Manifest Destiny and the search for opportunity in the great unknown. They were far from being a wealthy family. Harry's father had tried his hand at many careers before settling down as a farmer and livestock dealer; later in life he would serve as a road construction supervisor. They were the quintessential frontier family, building their lives brick by brick with the work of their hands and scratching a living from the fruit of the earth. It was this lifestyle of hard work and perseverance that would shape Harry's approach to life. He was always the sort to tackle issues head-on, with his sleeves rolled up. He was never afraid to get his hands dirty.

As he grew up on the American plains, Truman was a little different than other boys his age. Almost from birth, his vision was very poor, resulting in the need for him to wear glasses. At the time, this was very uncustomary; it would later become his trademark image. Because of this, his mother didn't like for him to rough house and play with other boys his age; they in turn gave him a hard time and often called him an owl because of his spectacles. He also felt very awkward around girls, despite being very outgoing. As a result, Truman's interests turned inward. He enjoyed reading, especially tales about military heroism. He also played the piano. As he grew older, he was torn between wanting to become a concert pianist or a famous soldier. Once, when interviewed by a reporter when he was president, Truman answered the question about becoming a politician with his usual good humor. "My choice early in life was either to be a piano player in a whorehouse or a politician. And to tell the truth, there's hardly any difference."

He worked diligently at his schoolwork, maintaining good grades all the way through high school. His goal, ultimately, was to go to West Point and earn a commission as an officer. From there he could fulfill his dreams of martial glory. To get there he worked hard in school, studying constantly and receiving very high marks in grade school and high school. Unfortunately for Harry, when he graduated and applied to West Point, he was not accepted due to his poor vision. Although he felt crestfallen with this decision, his father had run into financial problems, and he would have been unlikely to have been able to attend West Point. As it happened, the family finances were so dire that he was unable to attend a four year college after high school, and instead attended a business school in Kansas City. However, his family continued to suffer from financial distress, and after a semester, Harry left school and went to work for the mail room of the Kansas City Star in 1902.

Harry would earn his business education in the real world. After beginning at the Kansas City Star, where he would send money back to his family, he made the transition to working for a construction company. The work was better paying, and more befitted his hard working nature. The work was back breaking, but its results were much more visible. But his family needed more help financially, and the construction crew wasn't paying enough. Harry next moved up to a white collar job; he became a bank clerk. He worked hard and had a good head for figures from school. The money he earned was used to support himself in the big city. Everything he had left over was sent home. No matter how hard he worked, though, it never seemed to be enough. In 1906, after four years of trying to establish himself in the world, Harry decided to move back home and begin working on the family farm.

He worked on the farm with his brother Vivian. The work was hard, harder than when he had worked construction, but he had experienced it all throughout his childhood. Although it didn't bring in too much money and they barely made a profit, the farm was a guarantee of food for the family. It was in his blood. His family had been farmers since before they migrated into Missouri. The farm was his family's birthright, and there was a certain ownership Harry took in that, although it was not something he had ever wanted to do. He and his brother managed the farm during the term of his father's failing health, and it was long, grueling, tireless work. Somehow amid all the manual labor he had to perform Harry still found time to study, reading books and continuing his education without being in a formal university. He had always been scholarly, and he would continue his education throughout his life without ever attending a college.

Truman worked on and off at the farm for the next decade, but in 1905 he joined the National Guard. He had been denied acceptance into West Point due to his vision, but the National Guard in Missouri was much more accommodating. Growing up with stories about gallant deeds in battle, it was a lifestyle that Truman much admired, and he excelled at it. He continued his service to his country in the National Guard until 1916.

His father had passed away in 1914. This freed up a lot of commitment for him and his brother. Harry invested some of his money and became the owner and operator of a small mine. He did not meet with much success.

> The mine has gone by the board. I have lost out on it entirely. ..I shall endeavor to make the farm go as usual but I'll have to stay on it. My finances are completely exhausted...You would do better perhaps if you pitch me into the ash heap and pick someone with more sense and ability and not such a soft head.
>
> -Harry Truman

He was writing to Bess Wallace, a woman with whom he'd been talking for years. He had begun courting her in 1910. They were family friends, and had known each other since they were little. Harry tried his best, but despite his repeated confessions of love, Bess wouldn't take the bait. When he proposed marriage to her 1911, she rejected him. Despite this rejection, Truman did not give up in his courtship; he continued their romance until World War I.

Following his failed venture in mining, Harry turned next to drilling. The introduction of the automobile and the increased advances made by the Industrial Revolution had led to a boom in the oil industry; John D. Rockefeller had become the world's richest man through black gold. Harry was bound and determined to find similar success. Unfortunately, as geography and history have shown, Missouri is not dotted with a wealth of oil fields, and once again, Harry's foray into the business world met with negligible success.

These early failures, although frustrating, taught Harry humility. He knew that success in life was something that had to be worked at, not something that would be freely given, and it was this attitude of hard work and perseverance through life's obstacles that would characterize his involvement in World War I, and his entire political career. Unlike many scions of politics that were born into that high-ranking world, Harry had to scrape and claw his way into it using nothing but his determination and character.

Chapter 2

World War I

Carry the battle to them. Don't let them bring it to you.
Put them on the defensive and don't ever apologize for anything.

-Harry Truman

He sat around the table, listening to all the men in uniform making observations and recommendations. He felt very much like a fly on the wall, because none of these men were talking to him, or even at him. He was here at the behest of the President in order to be familiarized with ongoing operations. The men in uniform were talking to the President, seated in his wheelchair at the head of the table. Harry's invitation hadn't been by accident; it was widely whispered that Roosevelt was in poor health. Twelve years as President, a Great Depression, and a World War would do that to a person. Harry was there in the event that anything happened to the President.

He would need to know what was going on to maintain United States policies and operations.

Initially, he felt very much out of his depth. Code-named operations were being thrown around to a room of men who knew what they meant, troop deployments were being discussed, and the international political climate kept popping up. As he listened, it all began coming back to Harry. As they talked about the European Theater he could visualize the movement in his mind. He struggled a little more with the Pacific Theater and its obscure islands and atolls. He used the map on the wall for his benefit, and was then able to follow along with those events. As he listened he found himself getting caught up in it. War was a horrible thing, and this war was already the most destructive in human history, but there was an intricacy to it that couldn't be understood by the civilian. He had lived it, what seemed like a lifetime ago.

His attention for the conversation began to fade as he looked at the map of Europe. His mind tuned out the swastika showing Nazi controlled regions, and his eyes blurred the countless divisions arrayed against one another. In his mind he began to hear the howl of artillery, the typewriter sound of machine gun fire in the distance, and the continuous thunder of explosions.

His nose suddenly filled with the acrid smell of smoke, and he could envision gory bodies strewn across the barren waste of no-man's land. He closed his eyes, and a remembered skyline billowed smoke into the sky, its darkened swirls punctuated periodically by a bursting bombshell. He remembered the feeling of constant fear he felt, the uncertainty of it all, and the sense of duty to his men and his country. They were some of the strongest feelings he had felt in his life, all intensified by the constant death that had surrounded them.

A thundering fist on the table brought him back to the present. One of the military advisors to the President was talking about the war in the pacific and the tenacity of the Japanese defense. They had begun using a frightening tactic; pilots would use their fighters as a human guided missile, aiming themselves at United States warships and crashing into them. It was horrific, it was unprecedented, but it was also *bushido* – the warrior's code. The Japanese had been tougher than anticipated.

The meeting was drawing to a close, and a lot of emphasis was being placed on the state of the world after the war. It was in sight. The Axis powers were retreating on all fronts; the only question was how much longer it would take. Harry remembered similar discussions taking place between the Allied Powers after the First World War. It had been the war to end all wars, but the peace had been ineffective and served only as a catalyst for this present conflict.

During the First World War, he had played the role of soldier. He had commanded his men against the masses assembled by the Kaiser. He knew the terrors of war, and he knew the sweet bliss of peace. As his attention refocused on the meeting at hand, he knew how committed he was to establishing a strong and lasting peace. But when he looked at the map and saw the disposition of the various armies engaged in the conflict, he also knew that a future peace would involve more than just the defeat of the Axis threat.

World War I began in the late summer of 1914. In truth, it was a conflict that never needed to occur. For over one hundred years, Europe had plagued by a sense of rising nationalism, and European monarchies had fallen repeatedly to democratic revolutions. In some cases these revolutions occurred relatively peacefully. In most cases, they were horrific events that involved a lot of bloodshed. The nationalist movement in Serbia that was pushing for independence from Austria-Hungary was no different.

When Gavrilo Princip assassinated Archduke Ferdinand, he had had a limited idea of what his action would accomplish. He and his group, the Black Hand, had envisioned themselves cutting off the head of the future snake. But this was a local concept; the nationalist Serbians were not involved in the international discussions surrounding the "Balkan Question," and they did not understand the struggle over the balance of power in that region. They did not know the behind the scenes deals that had been made: Russia's support for Serbia, Germany's alliance with Austria-Hungary. The assassination of that one key figure was the first in a series of dominoes that would fall, leading to the largest war yet seen in human history.

After the assassination, Austria-Hungary reacted punitively, marching its armies into Serbia to subjugate the nationalistic terrorists who had put the royal succession in danger. When their armies mobilized, Russia declared its support and marched against Austria. This in turn triggered the defensive alliance between Germany and Austria-Hungary, and Germany declared war. Fearing the disruption of the balance of power in Europe, the United Kingdom and France came out in support of Russia, just as the Central Powers had known they would. Given Russia's immense size and the length of time needed to mobilize its military, and given the proximity of France, Germany focused first on France while Austria-Hungary dealt with the advanced elements of the Russian military. Europe had been preparing for war for the past fifty years, since the end of the Crimean War. Now, in less than a month, full scale war swept across the face of Europe, involving the majority of the most industrialized nations on Earth.

It was horrific. Modern technology made the war far more destructive than anyone could have imagined. Firearms could be produced on a grandiose scale following the Industrial Revolution, along with bullets and mortars. New, dreadful weapons made their way more explosively onto the scene, including things like machine guns, poison gas, airplanes, and tanks. Rather than kill men ten at a time, mankind had devised ways to kill thousands at a time.

It was the first truly modern war, it was the first truly industrial war, and it was the first truly global war. The imperial European powers called up soldiers from the far reaches of their empires. Foreign boys died on foreign sands, oftentimes in places they had never heard of before. The world had erupted in flame and destruction, and to many it seemed as if the end had finally come.

As the war etched its scars across Europe and the far-flung colonies, its effect was not felt in America. The United States had declined the invitation to join the Great War. In part, it was due to American foreign policy contained in the Monroe Doctrine. Mostly, it was due to the reluctance of the American government to send its citizens to die in a foreign conflict that had nothing to do with them. America traded with both nations, and America was not allied with either nation. America had no stake in the conflict, and therefore America preferred to stay isolationist.

Many Americans, however, felt like America needed to become involved. They saw the war as the great struggle of their lives, something they needed to participate in. Many American boys found their way to either Canada or England, where they could join in the struggle; although America hadn't chosen a side, it maintained deep cultural and economic ties with the United Kingdom. American isolation continued for the first three years of the conflict, but before long, following unprovoked German aggression in the Atlantic, it became clear that the United States would soon be drawn into the conflict. In 1917, before the United States officially entered the war, Harry S. Truman rejoined his National Guard unit, despite his age of thirty-three.

After the United States entered the war, Truman's National Guard was federalized and reorganized into the 129th Artillery Regiment. Truman, given the leadership he had demonstrated throughout his service in the

National Guard and his age and maturity, was made a captain and put in charge of Battery D.

When the United States had entered the war it was woefully unprepared for a conflict on such a scale. Compared to the armies that had been clashing in Europe, America's military was miniscule, and underwent rapid mobilization as the call to arms went out. Unfortunately, this meant it would take longer for the United States to join the conflict since it had to wait for its troops to be trained. Because they had already been consistently training as part of the National Guard, the 129th Artillery would see battle much sooner than many other Americans.

When he arrived in France, Truman quickly discovered that the soldiering life suited him. He had traveled to France ahead of his unit to gain extra training. He sat through briefings, he became familiarized with the disposition of friendly and enemy forces, and he was introduced to the new weapons of war he had not been exposed to. Once his men arrived, Harry was ready to lead them into battle. They would be part of a push including over 600,000 American soldiers who had arrived fresh to the war torn Western Front.

As he assumed command of his men in the face of such grisly dangers, he also discovered what he was made of. He was a natural born leader. He single handedly managed to whip into shape the men in Battery D who had a reputation for being unruly and ineffective, turning them into a top notch unit. He took control of his men and led them as they marched to meet the enemy. One of the first things they experienced was that war was all about movement.

"We sometimes went as far as 30 or 35 kilometers in a night," Harry had recorded in a letter home. In a war where success was measured in yards, it involved a lot of movement behind the scenes as the armies tried to mass their units for a decisive push in one location. Much of this marching was a case of hurry up and wait, as decisions were made higher up about where to push. Eventually, their marches brought them closer to the conflict, until suddenly they were in it.

> The whole front to our north broke out in flame, and a tremendous, continuous, and awe inspiring roar of artillery began; while huge searchlights, interspersed with many-starred signal rockets, shot their shafts like the Northern Lights constantly across the sky. We had heard or seen nothing in our experience like it.

Truman's words perfectly captured the shocking nature of the conflict, as well as the scale of it. For a boy from Missouri, it was both awe-inspiring and terrifying. As they reached the point of battle, his regiment received its orders. He and his men were to take up position within the Vosges Mountains. There, they were to concentrate their fire on the entrenched Germans. After they had fired their shots, the Germans answered with salvos of their own, sighted in by a German fighter plane overhead.

Truman thought this was the beginning of a gas attack, and ordered his men to put on their gas masks; they put theirs on, and then struggled to get masks onto the horses who hauled the artillery. In no time the shells began exploding around them. It was their first engagement; it was the first time they had seen combat. Many of his men broke and ran, frightened by the holocaust of flame and shrapnel exploding around them. Conversely, Truman stood his ground, watching his men turn to flee, and he ordered them back.

He would be the first to tell anyone that he had been just as frightened as they had been. In one incident later in life, he went so far as to describe himself as a bookworm, a sissy. Before leaving on the campaign he had made sure to bring extra glasses – 6 pair to be exact – because without them he was nearly blind. To get into the Army he had had to memorize the eye chart. He was no hero, but during the campaign at the Vosges Truman stood his ground and rallied his men. He hollered at them, he used every profanity he could think of, and he shamed them back into their positions.

They reluctantly returned, and continued their barrage against the Germans, eventually driving them back.

Following the battle at the Vosges Mountains, referred to by the men of Battery D as the "Battle of Who Ran," the 129th regiment was next ordered to the Argonnes. It was one of the most difficult marches of the entire war. The terrain they passed through was mountainous, rocky, and slick with the rains of autumn. Once they arrived, they became subsumed into the massive combined army of French, English, and American soldiers.

Truman gave the order to his men to fire at the same time the massive artillery barrage began. Over 4000 guns opened fire against the German lines. Their artillery barrages would be answered in turn by the enemy. Truman would comment at one point that being in the artillery was no picnic; soldiers shot at soldiers with bullets, but artillery fired at artillery with exploding shells and gas. As the battle raged on, Truman would experience his fair share of grisly death. As the Allied lines advanced slowly, Truman was able to observe firsthand the dreadful desolation of No Man's Land, possibly seeing craters in the ground that his Battery had created. The fight took a physical and emotional toll on him and his men, and it would be something that he would remember for the remainder of his life.

The battle of the Argonnes Forest would be one of the last major Allied offensives of the world, and would last from September 26th until the Armistice went into effect on November 11th. In the forty-seven days that the battle raged, Truman's Battery D would fire over 10,000 shells at the enemy. They fired their last shots fifteen minutes before the Armistice went into effect.

> When the firing ceased all along the front line it was so quiet it made me feel as if I'd been suddenly deprived of my ability to hear...We could hear the men in the

infantry a thousand meters in front raising holy hell. The French Battery behind our position were dancing, shouting, and waving bottles of wine. – Harry Truman

In a letter home to Bess, Truman captured the moment when the fighting stopped. The celebrating continued well into the night, and Truman claimed he was not able to get to bed until after two in the morning amid all the cheering and applauding and drinking. Truman's Battery D received very vocal praise from the French and British troops, and he and his men reveled in the abundance of cheap wine and food. They were celebrating success, they were celebrating victory. His men were celebrating him.

"We were just – well, part of it was luck and part of it was good leadership. Some of the other batteries didn't have that kind of leadership," commented Private Vere Leigh on one occasion, demonstrating the high regard his soldiers felt for Truman. Bookish though he might have been, he had led his men fearlessly into battle, sometimes into scathing fire, and would be returning most of them home. Truman had demonstrated his qualities as a soldier; he had also demonstrated his qualities as a leader.

Truman's service during World War I would greatly impact the remainder of his life. During the war, he had gained the ability to lead a group of men in the most demanding circumstances. It provided him with a much needed boost to his self-confidence after his mediocre career as a struggling farmer. He also emerged as a figure seen to be a leader; his men valued his skills and decisions, and he had made them into a cohesive unit. During the war, Truman had developed close friendships with some of his fellow soldiers, and these friendships would later form a significant basis for his political career. The war had given Truman's life a new meaning; he had found the martial glory he had always dreamed of as a child, and he had found a new direction in an otherwise directionless life. He had done his civic duty, and he would continue to perform this function for the remainder of his life

With the end of the war came the promise of something new; before leaving, Bess had told Harry that she wanted to get married, despite her previous refusal of his offer. Truman had asked her to wait, knowing full well the risks he would be facing. In a letter to her, he had told her "I don't think it would be right for me to ask you to tie yourself up to a prospective cripple – or a sentiment." He did go on to tell her how he felt about her, saying, "I'm crazy about you." Having survived the war in one piece, Truman would finally be able to fulfill his boyhood dreams of marrying Bess. He returned home, and on June 28, 1919, he married the love of his life in Independence, Missouri.

Chapter 3

Introduction to Politics

*I remember when I first came to Washington.
For the first six months you wonder how
the hell you ever got here. For the next six
months you wonder how the hell the rest
of them ever got here.*

- Harry Truman

It had quickly become apparent to Truman just how little power was placed into the hands of the Vice President. He was, for all intents and purposes, a bench warmer. He was a substitute. He was waiting in the wings in the event something happened to the President. He had attended meetings, he had been brought up to speed with ongoing operations of the war, but he was not involved in major policy discussions. No, Truman's job, if anything, was to champion the cause of the President, to help promote his agenda and rally American support to the war effort. With the conflict nearly completed, with the Axis powers against the rope, his job was very easy.

If Truman was being honest, he would have to say that being the Vice President was the easiest job he had ever had. It was also one of the most boring. Very little was required of him, and there were very few decisions he had to make. He hated feeling so useless; he was used to the feeling of hard work. As Vice President, he was more or less riding on someone's coat tails. And he understood the reason that the Founding Fathers had made the office so weak.

As the Vice President, he was technically the second most powerful person in the country, which would hypothetically give him a lot of power. This was dangerous; the wrong person in that office with the right public support could easily divide the country. So when the Constitution had been written, the responsibilities of the Vice President had been severely limited by law. He was in charge of Congress. For the rest, he was at the President's discretion. Ever since John Adams had filled that office, the message had been clear: the President was in charge, and the Vice President was largely a non-entity.

But Truman was determined to be an entity. He knew he was meant for more than failed businesses and local politics. He had served with distinction during the Great War, and he had demonstrated his political merits as he was faced with challenges like the Great Depression. He knew he had the head for it. Even though he had never been to college, he had learned from the school of hard knocks, the same way that many of America's greatest presidents had. He knew he had the background, and now he was poised on the precipice of greatness. He was not afraid to take the step. It was also not up to him.

On returning from the war, Truman once more ventured into the business world. During the war he had befriended a man named Eddie Jacobson. Shortly after marrying Bess, Truman teamed up with Eddie, and they opened a haberdashery. Truman knew that one of the keys to success was to dress for the job you were looking for, not for the job you had. He also figured thousands of returning vets would be thinking the same thing, and those men would need dress clothes. Truman and Jacobson took out several loans to get the business up and running, and for the first time in the business world, Truman was successful.

Through his store, Truman was introduced to several high ranking individuals in Kansas City. He was also able to stay in touch with the various acquaintances he had made in the Army and the National Guard. Because he was a respectable businessman, he had been invited to join civic organizations like the Triangle Club, which was made up of a group of businessmen dedicated to improving the city. As a military veteran, he was also able to join organizations like the American Legion and the Reserve Officers Association. Within the confines of these organizations, and through the continued patronage in his store, he was able to come in contact with a lot of highly influential people, while at the same time establishing a reputation as a respectable, hard-working, civic minded individual.

Despite the store's initial successes, though, there was a minor recession that took place right after war's end. This occurred for many reasons, from increased unemployment as soldiers returned home, to a declining amount of government spending into the economy. No matter the various causes, one result was certain: Truman's shop went out of business. What made matters worse was that he still had loans to repay. Truman took the failure of his business in stride, as he had with his numerous other failed ventures. He would have to move on to the next thing, and he would have to do it quickly. He still owed money for the loans he had borrowed.

Truman was like many Americans in the early 1920s, caught in the grip of easy credit and crippling debt. America had experienced an economic boom with World War I, and after a mild recession, was riding the wave of credit, speculation, and good times. It was the Roaring 20's, and Americans across the country were setting themselves up for failures that were similar to what Truman was experiencing.

Though his shop went out of business, Truman was able to keep up the network of friends and associates he had made through his organizations. This was fortunate. Rumors of Truman's respectability and work ethic had percolated through the ranks of Kansas City's political leadership, and in 1922, the same year that his haberdashery business had failed, he was approached with an offer he had never expected.

Thomas J. Pendergast, the democratic boss of Kansas City, was an uncle of one of Truman's friends from World War I. After hearing stories about Truman's leadership at the battles of the Vosges and Argonnes, and hearing Truman's name pop up in social circles, Pendergast believed that Truman would be an excellent choice for public office. More importantly, he believed that Truman's reputation for honesty and hard work would attract like-minded, independent voters. He could also count on Harry's fellow veterans to support him on Election Day. With these considerations in mind, he approached Harry and asked him if he would be interested in running for a judgeship on the county court of the eastern district of Jackson County. Truman, who had never considered a career in politics, was overwhelmed by the prospect, but accepted it graciously. After all, he had loans to pay off.

The race was close. There were five democratic candidates all vying for the same position in the primary. With Pendergast's support and his own charisma, Truman was able to win the primary election. He then went on to easily beat his Republican rival during the election in November. Harry Truman, a failed businessman and entrepreneur, a successful soldier, had become a politician.

His role as judge for the eastern district of Jackson County was a little misleading. He quickly found himself performing the functions of a county commissioner. Rather than judging court cases, Harry found himself working heavily with the county's budget and maintaining the roads. One function of his job that he despised was providing positions and contracts to individuals who supported Pendergast; along with that came talk of corruption and graft, which were unavoidable when working with Pendergast. Through all of that, Harry maintained his reputation for integrity and honesty. As he served, he held true to a statement he made when he was elected. "We intend to operate the county government for the benefit of the taxpayers. While we were elected as Democrats, we were also elected as public servants." His efficiency and dedication to his work appealed to his patrons in the Democratic Party, and his integrity endeared him to the voters of Jackson County.

Following a feud and division within the Kansas City Democratic Party, Harry lost re-election in 1924, but he continued campaigning and was re-elected in 1926, again with the help of the Pendergast political machine. This time he entered office as the presiding judge of the county court. In this position he was responsible for taking great steps in modernizing and rebuilding Jackson County's road system. He oversaw several important construction projects, and continued managing the county's finances, even as the United States began plunging into the first years of the Great Depression. He then won re-election in 1930. Harry S. Truman was becoming a political institution in Jackson County, Missouri. It was a conception envisioned by many:

> During these years of strenuous service to Jackson County he has found time to serve as president of the National Old Trails Association, an office he still holds. He has become widely known throughout Missouri, and many of his friends have expressed the opinion that he will fill the office of governor someday.

-Harry Truman

Although he was in office as part of the Pendergast political machine and had to reward the machine's political allies, Harry strove to make local governance as efficient and effective as possible. He earned a reputation of scrupulousness and for honest dealing, things which benefited Pendergast. Despite charges of corruption, Pendergast could point to Truman as an honest, clean judge, something not many politicians could earn a reputation for. Harry was a natural, and the people of Kansas City liked him. He was able to win support from a broad spectrum of voters, ranging from rural Americans to urban African-Americans and other ethnicities. Harry had the unique ability to bring people together and lead them.

His term as judge ended in 1934, and Truman decided to take the next step. He had found his calling; he was a dedicated public servant, and he had always been most successful when he was working as a public servant. After eight years establishing his reputation and honing his tradecraft, he was ready to climb the political ladder. In 1934, he asked Pendergast for his support. Truman wanted to run for a seat in the United States House of Representatives, and Pendergast agreed. At some point along the way, however, the People's Liberation Army changed. Harry was no longer running for a seat in the House of Representatives. Harry was running for a seat in the United States Senate.

The Primary was tough, especially on Harry, with his reputation for honor and integrity. There were widespread reports that the ballot boxes had been stuffed by Harry's supporters. Those same reports were also made about his competitors. At the end of the primary, Harry narrowly emerged as the Democratic candidate. When the election took place in November, Harry was easily able to beat the Republican candidate. In December, 1934, Harry, his wife Bess, and their daughter Margaret, packed their bags and moved to the nation's capital. When he arrives, Truman confessed that he felt "as timid as a country boy arriving on the campus of a great university for his first year."

Harry rose to the level of national politics as the United States was plunging into the depths of the Depression. Franklin Roosevelt had become president two years before, and he had been vigorously striving to put a stop to the Depression since he assumed office. He had told Americans he had a "New Deal," and the changes he had made to American politics had been new indeed. In his first years as a United States Senator, Harry supported several pieces of New Deal legislation passed by Roosevelt. Through this support, he emerged as a loyal supporter of Roosevelt's, as well as a powerful ally for labor unions. He got along well with the "good old boys" club within Congress, finding that network to be very similar to the networks of men he had belonged to after the war. He also played to his strengths; when he realized that most of the work in Congress was performed in committee rooms, he threw himself entirely into whichever committees he could.

Given his extensive practice in organizing the infrastructure within Jackson County, specifically with roads and budgeting, Truman made his mark on transportation issues as a member of the Appropriations Committee and the Interstate Commerce Committee. Along with the help of Senator Burton Wheeler, Harry wrote the Transportation Act of 1940, in an effort to untangle the regulations affecting transportation industries. He also helped created the Civil Aeronautics Act of 1938, which helped lead to the growth of the airline industry. As a first term senator, Harry was making quite a name for himself.

As his first term as senator drew to a close, Truman was facing a tougher election in 1940. In large part, this was because the political machine that had launched him to power, the Democratic machine led by Pendergast, had fallen apart. Pendergast himself was in prison, largely due to the charges of corruption. He was also ill. Harry would have to face this election all by himself, and win not with the political machine but by his own merit.

He was able to beat out the Missouri governor Lloyd Stark, but did so only by 8000 votes. He was able to pull out this small lead by reaching the citizens where Stark could not, in the urban and ethnic neighborhoods in Missouri's cities, demonstrating that Truman was a "candidate of the cities, an urban liberal."

In a nation where the cities had been the hardest hit by the Depression, Harry had emerged as a candidate of the people. It was an era where the people needed to know the individuals in government cared for them, and they had that with Truman.

Truman began his second term as a United States Senator at a precarious point. 1941 saw the United States on the verge of war. Nazi Germany had swept across Europe and North Africa, and the Japanese were turning the Pacific Ocean into a Japanese lake. Towards the end of 1940, Congress had appropriated ten billion dollars for defense and military spending. Truman convinced the Senate and President Roosevelt to make him the head of a special investigative committee designed to monitor and stop wasteful spending. This committee would become known as the Truman Committee, and it was slightly successful in stopping the graft. He championed it as a way to protect the little man from big, predatory businesses, and as a result it gained him increased popularity and recognition.

For most Americans, it had become common knowledge that the United States would soon enter the war. Britain was on its last legs, and the Soviet Union was being beaten back by the hammer of Nazi aggression. Although Truman represented his constituents by voting on the Neutrality Acts in the 1930s, he was aware of the threat that Germany, Japan, and Italy presented. In fact, once war erupted across Europe, he was one of the biggest supporters of the "cash-and-carry" and Lend-Lease policies presented by Roosevelt. As a former military man, he also supported the passage of the

Selective Service Act, as well as the efforts made at rearmament. When accused of flip-flopping on neutrality, Truman responded that "we are dealing with a bunch of thugs, and the only theory a thug understands is a gun and a bayonet."

Truman continued to serve at the forefront of his committee. It was his work investigating government spending and making sure that the funds were properly allocated that caused him to catch the eye of the senior Democratic Party leaders. He had saved taxpayers millions of dollars, and he had saved Roosevelt and the New Deal a lot of embarrassment by catching potentially damaging mistakes. His record as a senator began to conform more and more closely to the policies of Roosevelt, and as the 1944 election drew nearer, most Democrats agreed that Truman made a better Vice Presidential candidate than Henry Wallace, whose unpopularity with the Democratic Party had him on the outs. Through his tireless efforts in

Congress, Truman had been earmarked for the office of Vice President, to run on the ticket of Franklin Delano Roosevelt's fourth election.

Chapter 4

Vice President

It had been a flurry of activity. Harry was not one to let the grass grow under his feet, and he wasn't going to let his non-relationship with Roosevelt change that. He had been in the Senate for years, and he was very familiar with the procedures as well as the people there. Now he presided over that illustrious body, calling them to order and managing the proceedings of the day. He knew, as did most people, that it was almost a ceremonial position, that the Vice President wielded very little actual power over the Senate. But he was able to use his connections and knowledge to move things along very smoothly. With the war drawing to a close, there were major policy changes that were creeping up on the horizon.

As the Vice President, he would be responsible for helping to push through the President's agenda to the best of his ability. Luckily for Truman, he agreed with many of the

President's policies. He would be able to support the policies because he actually approved of them, and not because he was towing the party line. Besides, his communication with Roosevelt was minimal, and he received very little instruction on what to do. Roosevelt had bigger issues to concern himself with.

Harry was getting used to the role. It wasn't as bad as he had initially feared, and there was a fair amount of prestige that had come with the position. He was now one step away from becoming president of the United States; although he had enjoyed his time in the Senate, he would be lying if he said had never considered becoming the President of the United States. The President wasn't the picture of perfect health. The longer he had served as Vice President, the more he had heard whispers and seen just how much a toll the job had taken on Roosevelt's health. Some days he looked as if a stiff wind would blow him over, but he always managed to rally before giving a speech, or appearing on television. Roosevelt truly knew how to present himself to the people; in fact, Harry knew that most people outside of Washington D.C didn't even realize the President was paralyzed from polio. That's how successful a politician Roosevelt was. Harry wasn't sure if he would ever prove as tactful.

He had just adjourned the Senate for the day, as he had for the past eighty-two days. He was planning to meet with the Senate majority leader for drinks, as well as whatever political discussions happened to pop up. He was just about to leave his office when a secretary ran up and told him he was urgently needed at the White House. He gave instructions to cancel his lunch with his apologies, and then made his way to the White House. Thoughts swirled in his head. Had something happened in Europe? Had something happened in the Pacific? Had the war ended? It could have been anything, but whatever it was, it was important. The President had never sent for him urgently before. A smile crossed his face as he thought about how nice it was to finally be needed

Although it had been well discussed within the Democratic Party, it still came as a shock to Truman when he received the nomination. He had argued vehemently against the nomination, not wanting to put his family through the ordeal. Even his mother was against the idea, telling him to stay in the Senate. "The Vice President," she had said, "simply presides over the Senate and sits around hoping for a funeral." When he had been asked, Truman admitted that it was a high office, but also one that he did not aspire to. His secret hope was to become Senate Majority Leader. He did not know that Roosevelt had decided on him, because even Roosevelt had kept the selection secret so as not to alienate the other candidates.

When he was nominated, it had caught him off guard. Initially he declined the invitation, and it took the persuasion of the Democratic leadership and a phone call from

Roosevelt to convince him. "Well, you tell him that if he wants to break up the Democratic Party in the middle of the war, that's his responsibility," the President had said. Truman grudgingly accepted, but did comment, "Why the hell didn't he tell me in the first place?"

After he officially accepted the nomination as Vice President, Truman was beset with a host of accusations made by the Republican Party as well as by members within his own party. He was accused by some of being a member of the Ku Klux Klan, despite the fact that he had fought them continuously during his service in Jackson County. Some called him the "Little Man from Missouri," and others objected to the fact that Truman had placed his wife on his Senate payroll. He argued back, telling them that she had earned every penny. Despite these allegations and the mudslinging, most Americans preferred not to challenge a president in the middle of a war. Roosevelt had seen them through the grips of the Depression and had nearly navigated them through the Second

World War. They would vote for him regardless of who was on his ticket.

Despite being caught woefully unprepared for the national campaign, Truman performed with all his characteristic vigor during the national campaign. When the election came around in November, the Democratic ticket was able to handily defeat the Republican ticket. Franklin Delano Roosevelt had won his fourth presidential election, and on his coat tails into the White House went Harry S. Truman.

Truman would serve for a grand total of 82 days in the office of Vice President. Though it was a short period of time, he performed many pivotal functions for the president, despite their superficial relationship. Given his longstanding connection to the Senate, and his official Vice Presidential duty of presiding over the Senate, Truman served as a conduit between the White House and the upper house of Congress. He helped confirm the previous Vice President, Henry Wallace, as the new secretary of commerce, and he was able to block the Taft lend-lease amendment. This amendment would have forbidden the use of the lend-lease agreement for post-war relief to the war-ravaged allies of the United States. These policies he helped guide and push through the house were party policies, agendas influenced by the President, but Truman's support was accomplished because they were things Truman believed in. Although he had been selected by the President, his appointment had been a party decision, and his relationship to Roosevelt was nearly nonexistent. The President rarely reached out to him, and kept Truman in the dark about many aspects of the governance of the country, including the top secret Manhattan Project. During his term as Vice President, Truman and Roosevelt only met alone together twice. So distant was their relationship that, on seeing the President just before the national campaign, Truman was shocked by the gaunt appearance of the nation's leader.

The Vice Presidency was a brief chapter in the political life of Harry Truman. The President, who was no longer the image of fortitude and resilience he had been during the Depression, was in poor health. He had gone to Warm Springs, Georgia, as he often had, to take the waters. There, on April 12, 1945, Franklin Delano Roosevelt suffered a cerebral hemorrhage and passed away, leaving behind a legacy of service and an office of the American Presidency that was drastically different from when he had first assumed it twelve years before.

Harry, who had just adjourned the meeting of the Senate and was about to meet with the Majority leader, received a message that he was urgently needed at the White House. He had assumed it was because the President needed to see him, but on arriving he met Eleanor Roosevelt.

"Harry, the President is dead," she had told him.

Harry, stricken by the news, asked her, "Is there anything I can do for you?"

Eleanor looked at him with sympathy in her eyes and said to him, "Is there anything we can do for you? You are the one in trouble now!"

Shortly thereafter, Harry took the oath of office. He had just become the thirty-third president of the United States, and he assumed the office in the shadow of a giant.

Chapter 5

The President Who Dropped the Bomb

The atom bomb was no "great decision." It was merely
another powerful weapon in the arsenal of righteousness.

- Harry Truman

It had been a busy day of meetings and conferences and calls and decisions. Harry walked around the Oval Office, making his way over to the bar and pouring himself a glass of bourbon before he made his way to the plush chair and collapsed. He was exhausted; he never knew that a person could become so fatigued without doing manual labor. As he raised the glass to his lips, he reflected on his predecessor. It was no wonder his health had become so ragged. He had done this for over twelve years. Harry had only been in office for a few months, and all he wanted to do was curl up and go to sleep for a week. The burden of responsibility rested heavily on his shoulders. There was a lot of unfinished work to do, and Harry would be damned if he was going to mess up the progress that had been made under Roosevelt.

In Europe, the Allies were racing to Berlin. The war was all but over there, it was just a matter of when it would finish. Units in Europe were already being reassembled and shipped off to the Pacific to lend support to the island hopping campaign. Once Nazi Germany was eliminated, then the entire focus of the United States could be directed against Japan. The war's end was such a foregone conclusion that the allied leaders were already discussing what to do with the world once it emerged from the specter of war. The Yalta Conference had been a big step in this direction, but now that he was at the helm of the United States, Harry would need to meet with Churchill and Stalin and provide his own views.

Perhaps the biggest shock that had come to Truman was the revealing of something called the Manhattan Project. It had been conducted in absolute secrecy in the sparsely settled deserts of New Mexico, and was so tightly guarded that he hadn't even been made privy to it in his tenure as Vice President. Top scientists and physicists from around the world, including many Jewish expatriates who had fled Nazi Europe, had been working around the clock on a weapon based on Einstein's theory of relativity. Apparently, so the theory went, there was enough energy contained in a single atom that the explosive force unleashed by its being split would make traditional explosives obsolete. It read and sounded like science fiction, but based on recorded tests and video footage, it was stone cold reality.

Apparently the secrecy around the device was maintained because various other nations were working on a similar weapon. Many of the physicists now working on it had come from Germany, but it was widely known that the Nazis were developing all sorts of new technological weapons, trying to find a fix that would reset the scales in their favor. As far as American intelligence knew, however, the Germans had not yet unlocked Einstein's theory. No one had, except for the Americans.

Harry reclined his head into the cushion of the chair, savoring the taste of bourbon and the feeling of comfort. He glanced at the clock, noting that it was past one o'clock in the morning. He knew he had an early morning, and the one thing he had already learned as President was that a full night's sleep was not a guarantee. He finished the glass and set it on the table, and then stood and made his way to the living quarters. Once he changed into his night clothes and crawled into bed, he closed his eyes. No matter how hard he tried he could not stop seeing the explosive force of the atomic bomb blowing apart the beautiful sky over the New Mexico desert.

"Boys, if you ever pray, pray for me now. I don't know if you fellas ever had a load of hay fall on you, but when they told me what happened yesterday, I felt like the moon, the stars, and all the planets had fallen on me." On hearing that the President had died, Truman suddenly felt that he carried the weight of the world on his shoulders. Worse, Roosevelt's great agendas had been left unfulfilled. The Great Depression had only ended with the surge of American government spending during the war, Truman would need to make sure that the new policies that had been put in place were able to prevent the post-war recession that would inevitably occur. Roosevelt's leadership had also brought America to the brink of victory, but being this close to the finish line did not guarantee that America would cross it. That burden was now Harry's. And, in typical Truman fashion, he rolled up his sleeves and committed to getting the job done.

Though he lacked the oratorical skills and the striking figure of Roosevelt, Truman possessed many skills that the American people loved. He was known to be a hard working individual, and he was also known for his honesty, even when surrounded by individuals who were not. Truman was also capable of making difficult decisions; many claimed that he delighted in the act, as if it affirmed his commitment to the American people. When he made a decision, it was what he thought was in the best interest of the country. He did not cast votes based on passing popularity or infamy. He was a public servant, and his job was to serve the public.

On assuming the office of President, he asked Roosevelt's cabin to remain in place while he got situated. He wanted to maintain a consistency of policy as he familiarized himself with the strings of power, and those individuals were intimately familiar with the late President's policies both at home and abroad. Though he had attended a few meetings, Truman had been left largely in the lurch as the Vice President. However, by late spring, he was comfortable enough to begin cleaning house and replacing Roosevelt's cabinet with people of his own choosing. Most were men whose names no one had heard, and his appointee to the office of Attorney General resulted in a corruption scandal that marred Truman's popularity.

Once in the office, Truman began to appreciate just how much the office of President had been transformed by Roosevelt. The President was now flanked by a host of staff members and cabinet members, was inundated by a steady flow of information, and led by delegation. In short, the responsibilities that had been assumed by Roosevelt into the office had grown so much that no one man could do the job. He needed a team of loyal members, as well as a chief of staff who could dedicate himself to the running of the White House. Truman, however, did not want to give up control of the driving car he had jumped into, and he remained largely his own chief of staff during his first term as President.

One month after taking office, news reached the United States that Adolph Hitler had entered a bunker under Berlin. There, he and his mistress Eva Braun had committed suicide. The Third Reich was now leaderless, and soon it crumbled. The Allied Powers were able to celebrate Victory in Europe day on May 8, 1945. Two months later, the Allied leaders met in Potsdam, Germany, to discuss the division of the postwar world. The world was emerging from one fight, and already had the next conflict in sight. Two conflicting ideologies, Capitalism and Communism, were already beginning to tear at the fragile end strings of the world. In Potsdam, the leaders had gathered to discuss spheres of influence, but as they met, there was one trump card that only Truman knew about. The United States had successfully constructed and tested the world's first atomic bomb, claimed to be "the most terrible weapon ever known in human history." Though he was new and inexperienced in political discussion when it came to such figures as Churchill and Stalin, Truman's knowledge of the weapon enabled him to negotiate more powerfully for American interests overseas.

Truman returned home from the conference having successfully asserted America's role in the emerging world. The United States had traditionally been an isolationist nation, drawn into conflicts only when provoked. But out of the Allied Powers, the United States was the only one relatively untouched by war. The United Kingdom, France, the Soviet Union, and China, had all been destroyed by years of warfare. America was in an unexpected position of power; unknown to the other nations, it was also the only country on earth with the atomic bomb.

The War in the Pacific was drawing to a close, but Japanese tenacity in the defense of their homeland was clearly demonstrated. Kamikaze pilots had taken to the sky, using their planes as guided missiles as they went on suicidal runs, targeting American battleships. Old men, women, and children, were being drilled with wooden weapons to fight back the American invaders. When the American marines captured the island of Okinawa, civilians threw themselves from the cliffs, committing mass suicide rather than be captured. And the battles were grisly.

When the United States captured Iwo Jima, it had been at the cost of 26,000 American casualties. When Okinawa had fallen, it had cost an additional 72,000 casualties. These numbers had occurred while attacking small, outlying islands. Now, American military planners were looking at a full scale invasion of Japan itself as the only way to force the Japanese to unconditionally surrender. As they considered the grim determination of the Japanese, their code of bushido, and the number of soldiers that would be committed to battle, they came to the conclusion that the invasion of Japan would be horribly costly. When Truman received the reports, the casualty figures ranged from 200,000 to 500,000 American lives. No matter what ways the strategists changed their predictions, there was no avoiding the grisly cost of an invasion of Japan. But Truman knew something they didn't know.

On August 6, 1945, an old B-29 bomber named the Enola Gay took off from an airfield in the Mariana Islands carrying a cargo the world had never seen before. At 8:15 in the morning, Hiroshima time, a bomb named Little Boy was dropped on the city of Hiroshima. After falling for 43 seconds, the bomb detonated slightly above ground level; the effect was devastating. The bomb detonated with a force of 16 kilotons, and the blast radiated out over one mile in diameter, destroying everything within. In all, nearly five square miles of city were destroyed, and nearly 100,000 people were incinerated. The news was received by the rest of the world with stunned silence; the destructive force of one single weapon had been unimaginable. The United States had ushered the world into the Atomic Age.

Following the blast, word was carried to the Japanese Emperor demanding his nation's unconditional surrender. Because the surrender was unconditional and involved the Emperor being handed over to stand trial despite his godlike status, and owing to the Japanese warrior code of bushido, the surrender offer was rejected. On August 9, 1945, a second atomic bomb was dropped on Japan, this time one the industrial city of Nagasaki. The United States planned to continue its atomic bombing campaign in Japan, but the Japanese had seen the destruction these weapons could cause. They knew that to continue the fight would not only obliterate the Japanese civilization, but could also destroy mankind. Japan officially announced its surrender on August 14, 1945, and then more officially signed the terms of surrender on September 2. The most devastating war in human history had been brought to an end.

Historians have argued over the countless possible reasons Harry S. Truman ordered the dropping of the atomic bomb; undoubtedly all are probably correct in one fashion or another. Traditionalists will say that Truman ordered the dropping of the bomb to save as many American lives as he could. Any President would do the same if given the same circumstances. Apologists will say that the bomb was dropped as part of a Machiavellian scheme to demonstrate to the nations of the world the authority with which America now negotiated. The decision to drop the bomb did come after Stalin had finally agreed to send his soldiers against Japan and the Soviet Union had declared war on Japan, which has caused some to see it as American sabre rattling, which it possibly was. The United States and the Soviet Union were already fighting the battle of influence before the embers of war had burned out. Regardless of the reason, or reasons, for which the bomb was dropped, the decision to drop it would have lasting implications on the world. It had ended World War II, it had thrust the United States into the forefront of international relations, a position it had never held before, and it ushered in an era of military buildup. Unbeknownst to everyone at the time, the dropping of the atomic bombs would be the first block laid in the foundation of the Cold War.

Chapter 6

The United States and the Postwar World

*"A pessimist is one who makes difficulties of his opportunities
and an optimist is one who makes opportunities of his difficulties."*

\- Harry Truman

The war had drawn to a close. The atomic bomb had been successful, and the effect it had had on America's postwar negotiations was staggering. On the one hand, mused Truman, he was happy to have the authority of the weapon, as it made his job that much easier. On the other hand, it had distinct disadvantages. It had catapulted the United States into a previously unsought position of world leader. In the past, the United States had played the role of world power. It was comfortable with its industry and wealth and the fighting spirit of its soldiers, but the United States had never sought notoriety on the level that would result in influencing global decisions.

World War II had ended that distinction. This was in large part due to the fact that nearly every other nation on earth had been scarred by the ravages of war. Aside from the military casualties and material losses, Americans had been lightly impacted at home by the war. Cities did not need to be rebuilt; new jobs did not need to be created. America was the only truly industrialized nation that did not have to start over from scratch. It had become a world leader almost by default, even though the atomic bomb did help.

This meant that he would now play a larger role on the world stage than had ever been envisioned. Perhaps Roosevelt had seen it, had seen what would happen, and perhaps Roosevelt would have been more prepared for that. But Harry was a man from Missouri, not college educated, not accustomed to dealing with world leaders. It was a skill he would have to learn, and learn quickly. Luckily for Harry, any time he applied himself in politics, he succeeded. He hoped this time would be no different.

There was a lot to consider in this postwar world. America was a country with vast resources while the remainder of the world had little. Trade with European nations had dropped off as a result of the war, and this recession would likely continue as those nations struggled to find the finances to rebuild. The financial problem was insignificant in relation to the major problem facing the postwar world. As nations had toppled and empires fell, power vacuums across the world were emerging. Revolutions had sprung up against colonial powers, and political groups fought for control in countries where power structures no longer existed. As new governments assumed the reins of power, they had a host of political ideologies to choose from. At the moment, two were in vogue: democracy and communism.

As the thirty-third president of a free society, where he had been elected by the will and consent of the people, Truman was biased towards democracy. Communism was a cheap knock off, where too much power was placed in the hands of the government. As Abraham Lincoln had said, "Power corrupts; absolute power corrupts absolutely." No matter how high minded and noble the ideas of communism had been, it was a system that could not work. Looking at the Soviet Union, it was easy to see the subjugation experienced by the population, the squalor in which they lived. Truman did not want to see the nations of the world succumb to that horror, nor did he want it to fall into anarchy. He saw democracy as the natural choice. He believed the arguments of the Founding Fathers and the political philosophers who had inspired them. People should have a stake in the government that represents them.

More importantly, governments tended to ally themselves to nations with similar governments. The more countries that could be convinced to embrace democracy would mean there would be more countries willing to embrace the United States in friendship. In its new role of world power, the United States would need as many friends as it could get, and Harry had the distinct advantage of being the strongest kid on the block.

Europe was in shambles. Six years of warfare which included continual artillery barrages, explosions intended to make roads impassable, and aircraft bombing runs involving thousands of planes and millions of warheads would do that to a place. Japan was even worse, with its delicate wooden structures that could little resist the fire-bombing and nuclear explosions which had laid waste to its countryside. In both locations, they were the unfortunate exigencies of war, the cost of doing battle. The death and destruction represented the loss of huge percentages of population, and even larger percentages of infrastructure. The United States, by comparison, was virtually untouched, and was now faced with a world that needed to be rebuilt.

The process began with the division of Germany. Responsible for two World Wars, the country now found itself under allied occupation. The nation was divided among the four major powers that had fought against it, and the capital of Berlin was further subdivided. Armies from the four nations were stationed in Germany to prevent any future national uprising, or any attempt to resuscitate the Third Reich. Before the occupation began, the discussion over political ideology had already begun. It had been discussed at Yalta among the Big Three, and then later at Potsdam. No firm agreement had been reached, and slowly the occupied territories began to fall into the patterns and traditions of the nations occupying them. In West Germany, the area occupied by France, the United Kingdom, and the United States, a democratic form of government emerged. Conversely, In Soviet controlled East Germany, a totalitarian form of government in league with the Soviet Union formed. Germany, who had been the provocateur of two international conflicts, already appeared to be ground zero for the Third World War.

Japan, on the other hand, was solely occupied by the United States. This was because the United States had fought the Japanese virtually alone in the conflict. Asia had always been an extension of politics for the civilized world as all nations struggled to gain a foothold in the exotic market. In the early 1900s, China had been divided into spheres of influence between Russia, the United Kingdom, Germany, France, and the United States. Japan had been closed to European and American imperialism, before undergoing the Meiji Restoration which placed it on the path to World War II. Japan had conquered vast swaths of China, expelling many of the European nations. Now that the war was done, Japan's doors were flung open to trade with the United States. Despite its crippling defeat at the hands of the Americans, Japan prospered greatly under United States occupation. It also developed a form of democratic government similar to England's;

after all, the Emperor was a deity and could not simply be pushed aside. A constitutional monarchy, however, was far preferable to complete obedience to a single individual. With a new form of government, a capitalistic economy, and a hungry trade partner in the United States, a new ally was born from the ashes of an enemy. Japan had become an American foothold in Asia.

In a world destroyed by war and divided by politics, the one necessity was money. Money would buy food, housing, and infrastructure. It would buy anything that was necessary to relieve the struggle faced by the displaced citizens of a nation, and the United States and Soviet Union attempted to take advantage of that. Sometimes friends could be won by being yourself; sometimes friends could simply be bought.

In an effort to prevent Western Europe from collapsing under the neighboring weight of communist Russia, a plan was proposed by Secretary of State George C. Marshall and fully endorsed by Truman. It called for the United States to spend $13 billion, or roughly $130 billion in today's money, in an effort to help rebuild war torn Europe. There were many benefits to this plan. The first was that it would help speed along European recovery, which had been occurring much slower than anticipated. Once the nations of Europe were back on their feet, the second benefit would manifest as trade resumed between the United States and Europe, benefiting all parties involved. Lastly, and perhaps most importantly, it was hoped that the money used in the Marshall Plan would assist in the recruitment of American allies. After all, everyone likes a person who gives them money.

Under the Marshall Plan, money was given to European nations to help them rebuild in the postwar world. More money was given to nations that had been involved in World War II and had not been members of the Axis powers. On accepting this money, these nations also pledged their commitment to fighting the spread of communism within their borders.

To the United States, the Marshall Plan offered various distinct benefits. The first was the intended consequence, as European economies turned around and experienced revitalization with the aid of American money. The second was the extra money the United States earned as a result of the repayment of these loans. The United States was capitalizing both on interest from the Marshall Plan loans as well as the loans being paid under the terms of the Lend-Lease agreement. But most importantly, by funding European nations with the money from the Marshall Plan, the United States had gained expansive influence in Western Europe.

Due to proximity, as well as their involvement with the Axis powers, many nations in Eastern Europe did not receive the support of the United States, and were instead helped through the postwar rebuilding by the Soviet Union. Europe had been divided in the middle of two global wars; now it was divided by political beliefs.

Tensions escalated when the Soviet Union attempted to put pressure on the Western Allies.

In a show of force, the Soviet Union closed all entrances to its borders into Berlin. Berlin was divided between the four Allied powers from World War II, but Berlin itself sat in the zone occupied by the Soviet Union. When the Soviet Union closed its access points, it meant that the western powers could not enter or exit Berlin. It was a very heavy handed approach to international relations, and it left the Western powers with very few options but to deal.

Harry Truman was not going to be brow beaten by the Soviets. He was not going to give into their demands, nor was he going to risk open warfare. The Soviets had believed those were the only two options available when they closed the borders, but Truman believed he had found an answer to the problem. He consulted with his cabinet, with his staff, and most importantly with the leaders of Western Europe. The borders on the ground were closed, but there was another way.

The Berlin Airlift began in 1948. Called Operation Vittles by the Western Powers, rations were flown into the three major airports in the Allied zone at a rate of over 5,000 tons per day. Originally it was expected to be an operation of short duration. The Soviet Union had instigated the blockade claiming that the German Autobahn would be closed for repairs. After the Allies began airlifting supplies into Berlin, the Soviet Union was not ready to concede defeat. Undeterred by the lack of Soviet surrender on the issue of the blockade, the Allies continued sending in supplies for over a year. By the end of 1949, the Soviet Union was ready to declare that the blockade of Berlin had failed. The Allies had sent over 300,000 missions into the capital of Germany, dropping over 2.3 million tons of cargo during the operation. It was one of the first clashes between communism and democracy. It would not be the last.

Decades later, things would heat up around Berlin once again. Before long, a new division would stretch across Europe, this one much more tangible than political ideology. Displaced Europeans, most Germans, had been roaming the continent as refugees seeking new places to call home. As the Soviet Union took control over Eastern Germany, Germans became increasingly disaffected with the quality of the occupation, and began moving towards the Western Occupation Zone. For the Soviet Union, this was very bad publicity; it simply didn't look good to have a group of citizens massively exit your country. In order to prevent this movement, as well as prevent the cultural diffusion of democratic ideas into its communist society, the Soviet Union developed a new plan.

In the early hours of August 13, 1961, German citizens awoke to find a wall constructed down the middle of Berlin. The wall had been constructed back in the Soviet Union, and all the parts had been shipped so as to be erected at the same time. Over time, additions would be made to this wall until it stretched from the Baltic Sea in the north to the Mediterranean Sea in the South. Depth and layers would be added to the wall to make it more difficult to cross, and it would eventually be patrolled by guards and by dogs. The Soviet Union claimed that this was to prevent the Western powers from invading and corrupting their population, but the Western world knew different. The only places that built walls and patrolled those walls with guards and dogs were prisons.

In the East, the United States had near autonomy in Japan as it helped the island nation to rebuild. This upset the Soviet Union, as it reduced their sphere of influence in the region, more so given the Russian defeat in the Russo-Japanese War in the early 1900s. But the Soviet Union had played little part in the defeat of that Axis nation, and therefore had no claim in occupying it and guiding its political future. As it stood, the Soviet Union had its own plans in Asia, as did the United States.

The Japanese occupation of China had been brutal, causing a rupture in the government that was already weak due to its lack of legitimacy. The early twentieth century had seen numerous revolutions take place in China as dynasties crumbled and provisional governments failed. The nationalistic, democratic government led by Chiang Kai-Shek had been supported during the Second World War by the United States. Also fighting against the Japanese had been the communist guerilla forces led by Mao Zedong. When the war had ended, both leaders began fighting one another over what political future was in store for China. After long campaigning and tenacious battles, the communist armies of Mao were able to sweep aside the democratic resistance of Chiang Kai-Shek. The United States had its foothold in Asia through Japan; the Soviet Union settled for China, the most populated nation on earth.

The world after World War II was scarcely better than the old. Nations were still squabbling over power, and the world was becoming polarized in its viewpoints. For a while the United States held a distinctive edge. But in 1949, the Soviet Union closed the gap. On August 29, 1949, the Soviet Union successfully tested its first atomic bomb. The United States was no longer alone; the Arms Race had begun

Chapter 7

The Iron Curtain and the Truman Doctrine

You can always amend a big plan, but you can never expand a little one. I don't believe in little plans. I believe in plans big enough to meet a situation we can't possibly foresee now.

- Harry Truman

Truman was anxious. It had been a while since he had seen the Prime Minister from England, but they had been in touch nearly continuously since the end of the war. They had worked tirelessly to organize the United Nations. Sir Winston Churchill had lost his bid for re-election as Prime Minister in 1945. In part it was a relief after the stress of guiding his nation through the terrible days of World War II, the Battle of Britain, and the continued threat of Nazi conquest resting a mere boat ride away. Churchill suddenly found himself with time on his hands, lending itself to travel opportunities and book writing. Despite the loss of the election, however, Churchill was still an important figure in Britain. More importantly, you can take the man out of politics, but you can't take the politics out of the man.

Churchill had arrived to the United States with much fanfare and applause. Americans were happy to welcome the figure who had rallied his nation in its darkest hour, the man who had stood his nation alone against Hitler until the United States finally joined the war. Now this foreign dignitary was visiting the United States at the special request of the President, to maintain the strong ties that had been forged through the crucible of two World Wars. He had arrived at Westminster College in Fulton, Missouri, in a large official motorcade. Here in the President's home state, Churchill was preparing to give a speech that would fundamentally shape the world for the next generation.

Truman smiled warmly as Churchill emerged from the vehicle. He approached the

British bulldog and shook his hand, both men posing as reporters snapped their pictures. The crowd cheered and applauded. They exchanged small pleasantries as Churchill was shown to the stage where he could deliver his speech. There had been some discussion as to what would be discussed, but most of Churchill's speech was a mystery to the President.

Truman stood on stage while Churchill delivered his speech. He had spoken with the man countless times on the phone and in person, but none of those could compare to his delivery. Churchill was a magnificent speaker, using his voice to draw the audience in, building to the point, then letting the message burst over the crowd. He spoke with passion, he spoke with certainty, and he spoke intelligently. His was a voice the people could trust, just as the British had pledged their support when he had vowed they would "fight on the beaches, we shall fight on the landing grounds...we will never surrender." His was a voice that unified a people.

As Truman listened, he vaguely wished he had such a voice.

The speech drew to a close and the audience roared their approval. So did the United States government. This speech had demonstrated the growing threat of the Soviet Union against the peace of the world. Truman shared a similar belief, having met with Stalin. It also hadn't been forgotten among the allies that the Soviet Union had initially sided with Nazi Germany; the end of one war didn't mean the Soviet Union wouldn't consider a future one to acquire new territories. Truman agreed completely with Churchill. The Soviet Union needed to be stopped from its attempts at global domination.

With the detonation of the atomic bomb, the world had entered into the atomic age. In one instant, every other weapon on earth had been rendered obsolete. Despite emerging from World War II as the world's richest and strongest country, that one device made the United States the most powerful nation on earth by default. No one else had one. For the United States, this was a blessing and a curse. As a blessing, it gave the nation an opportunity to champion the ideas of freedom and democracy throughout the world. It gave the United States a global importance it had never had before, making it not simply *a* world leader, but *the* world leader. Despite the strength of the Allied Powers, they had been destroyed by war. America was glisteningly clean and untouched. The curse of this sudden rise to power was resentment, as nations which had existed for hundreds or thousands of years were suddenly overshadowed by a young idealistic upstart.

It is the unfortunate nature of nations to be distrustful and wary of one another. This occurs because of differences in culture, language, customs, and ethnicities. Nations are composed of people, and people tend to distrust that which is unfamiliar to them, especially when the thing that is different is suddenly more powerful. The Soviet Union looked on the United States and saw it occupying the place of prominence it deserved. The Soviet Union was the largest nation on earth. The Soviet Union had broken the back of the Third Reich as wave after wave of Nazi armies died in the frozen wastes fighting the tenacious Russians. It had been the Soviet Union who had bled Germany of the troops necessary to stop the D-Day Invasion, who had killed the experienced troops. Then came the United States, racing to capture the glory of the capture of Berlin, and then destroyed cities in the blink of an eye. The Soviet Union was envious of the position of the United States.

The United States, with its capitalist economy which fueled the class struggle the Soviet Union wanted to end. The United States, with its democracy and freedom of the press, which challenged government control of the means of production. To the Soviet Union, the United States was just as much a threat as Nazi Germany had been. The ideals of the United States could threaten everything the Soviet

Union had built, and now the United States was in a position to exert this authority. To counteract this threat, the Soviet Union began assimilating the collapsed nations of Eastern Europe into its Soviet folds. In order to counter the threat from the United States, the Soviet Union would have to gain influence by spreading and absorbing other nations.

This move was witnessed by the Western Powers. The aggression of the Soviet Union as it swallowed up nations like Latvia, Estonia, as its tendrils reached into nations like Poland, did not go unnoticed. The Soviet Union was marching into territories and annexing them exactly like Hitler had done just before the onset of World War II. The war hadn't even been over for a year, and already a new threat to the stability of the world was manifest.

After losing his re-election bid for Prime Minister, Sir Winston Churchill was invited to the United States to give a speech at Westminster College. Although he did not speak in an official capacity for the United Kingdom, his speech nonetheless carried the weight of the beliefs of that government, as well as for the United States. Truman agreed whole-heartedly with the speech given by Churchill, and he strongly believed the Soviet Union presented an even greater threat to the security of the world than Nazi Germany ever had. The speech given by Sir Winston Churchill would be the bedrock on which Truman would build the foundation of his presidential policies. It is with agreement and resolve that Truman listened to these words as Sir Winston Churchill spoke them:

I can therefore allow my mind, with the experience of a lifetime, to play over the problems which beset us on the morrow of our absolute victory in arms, and to try to make sure with what strength I have that what has been gained with so much sacrifice and suffering shall be preserved for the future glory and safety of mankind.

The United States stands at this time at the pinnacle of world power. It is a solemn moment for the American Democracy. For with primacy in power is also joined an awe-inspiring accountability to the future. If you look around you, you must feel not only the sense of duty done but also you must feel anxiety lest you fall below the level of achievement. Opportunity is here now, clear and shining for both our countries. To reject it or ignore it or fritter it away will bring upon us all the long reproaches of the after-time. It is necessary that constancy of mind, persistency of purpose, and the grand simplicity of decision shall guide and rule the conduct of the English-speaking peoples in peace as they did in war. We must, and I believe we shall, prove ourselves equal to this severe requirement.

When American military men approach some serious situation they are wont to write at the head of their directive the words "over-all strategic concept." There is wisdom in this, as it leads to clarity of thought. What then is the over-all strategic concept which we should inscribe today? It is nothing less than the safety and welfare, the freedom and progress, of all the homes and families of all the men and women in all the lands. And here I speak particularly of the myriad cottage or apartment homes where the wage-earner strives amid the accidents and difficulties of life to guard his wife and children from privation and bring the family up in the fear of the Lord, or upon ethical conceptions which often play their potent part.

To give security to these countless homes, they must be shielded from the two giant marauders, war and tyranny. We all know the frightful disturbances in which the ordinary family is plunged when the curse of war swoops down upon the bread-winner and those for whom he works and contrives. The awful ruin of Europe, with all its vanished glories, and of large parts of Asia glares us in the eyes. When the designs of wicked men or the aggressive urge of mighty States dissolve over large areas the frame of civilised society, humble folk are confronted with difficulties with which they cannot cope. For them all is distorted, all is broken, even ground to pulp.

When I stand here this quiet afternoon I shudder to visualise what is actually happening to millions now and what is going to happen in this period when famine stalks the earth. None can compute what has been called "the unestimated sum of human pain." Our supreme task and duty is to guard the homes of the common people from the horrors and miseries of another war. We are all agreed on that.

Our American military colleagues, after having proclaimed their "over-all strategic concept" and computed available resources, always proceed to the next step - namely, the method. Here again there is widespread agreement. A world organisation has already been erected for the prime purpose of preventing war, UNO, the successor of the <u>League of Nations</u>, with the decisive addition of the United States and all that that means, is already at work. We must make sure that its work is fruitful, that it is a reality and not a *sham, that it is a force for action, and not merely a frothing of words, that it is a true temple of peace in which the shields of many nations can someday be hung up, and not merely a cockpit in a <u>Tower of Babel</u>. Before we cast away the solid assurances of national armaments for self-preservation we must be certain that our temple is built, not upon shifting sands or quagmires, but upon the rock. Anyone can see with his eyes open that our path will be difficult and also long, but if we persevere together as we did in the two world wars - though not, alas, in the interval between them - I cannot doubt that we shall achieve our common purpose in the end.*

I have, however, a definite and practical proposal to make for action. Courts and magistrates may be set up but they cannot function without sheriffs and constables. The United Nations Organisation must immediately begin to be equipped with an international armed force. In such a matter we can only go step by step, but we must begin now. I propose that each of the Powers and States should be invited to delegate a certain number of air squadrons to the service of the world organization. These squadrons would be trained and prepared in their own countries, but would move around in rotation from one country to another. They would wear the uniform of their own countries but with different badges. They would not be required to act against their own nation, but in other respects they would be directed by the world organisation. This might be started on a modest scale and would grow as confidence grew. I wished to see this done after the First World War, and I devoutly trust it may be done forthwith.

It would nevertheless be wrong and imprudent to entrust the secret knowledge or experience of the atomic bomb, which the United States, Great Britain, and Canada now share, to the world organisation, while it is still in its infancy. It would be criminal madness to cast it adrift in this still agitated and un-united world. No one in any country has slept less well in their beds because this knowledge and the method and the raw materials to apply it, are at present largely retained in American hands. I do not believe we should all have slept so soundly had the positions been reversed and if some Communist or neo-Fascist State monopolised for the time being these dread agencies. The fear of them alone might easily have been used to enforce totalitarian systems upon the free democratic world, with consequences appalling to human imagination. God has willed that this shall not be and we have at least a breathing space to set our house in order before this peril has to be encountered: and even then, if no effort is spared, we should still possess so formidable a superiority as to impose effective deterrents upon its employment, or threat of employment, by others. Ultimately, when the essential brotherhood of man is truly embodied and expressed in a world organisation with all the necessary practical safeguards to make it effective, these powers would naturally be confided to that world organisation.

Now I come to the second danger of these two marauders which threatens the cottage, the home, and the ordinary people - namely, tyranny. We cannot be blind to the fact that the liberties enjoyed by individual citizens throughout the British Empire are not valid in a considerable number of countries, some of which are very powerful. In these States control is enforced upon the common people by various kinds of all-embracing police governments. The power of the State is exercised without restraint, either by dictators or by compact oligarchies operating through a privileged party and a political police. It is not our duty at this time when difficulties are so numerous to interfere forcibly in the internal affairs of countries which we have not conquered in war. But we must never cease to proclaim in fearless tones the great principles of freedom and the rights of man which are the joint inheritance of the English-speaking world and which through Magna Carta, the Bill of Rights, the Habeas Corpus, trial by jury, and the English common law find their most famous expression in the American Declaration of Independence.

All this means that the people of any country have the right, and should have the power by constitutional action, by free unfettered elections, with secret ballot, to choose or change the character or form of government under which they dwell; that freedom of speech and thought should reign; that courts of justice, independent of the executive, unbiased by any party, should administer laws which have received the broad assent of large majorities or are consecrated by time and custom. Here are the title deeds of freedom which should lie in every cottage home. Here is the message of the British and American peoples to mankind. Let us preach what we practise - let us practise what we preach.

I have now stated the two great dangers which menace the homes of the people: War and Tyranny. I have not yet spoken of poverty and privation which are in many cases the prevailing anxiety. But if the dangers of war and tyranny are removed, there is no doubt that science and co-operation can bring in the next few years to the world, certainly in the next few decades newly taught in the sharpening school of war, an expansion of material well-being beyond anything that has yet occurred in human experience. Now, at this sad and breathless moment, we are plunged in the hunger and distress which are the aftermath of our stupendous struggle; but this will pass and may pass quickly, and there is no reason except human folly of sub-human crime which should deny to all the nations the inauguration and enjoyment of an age of plenty. I have often used words which I learned fifty years ago from a great Irish-American orator, a friend of mine, Mr. Bourke Cockran. "There is enough for all. The earth is a generous mother; she will provide in plentiful abundance food for all her children if they will but cultivate her soil in justice and in peace." So far I feel that we are in full agreement.

Now, while still pursuing the method of realizing our overall strategic concept, I come to the crux of what I have travelled here to say. Neither the sure prevention of war, nor the continuous rise of world organization will be gained without what I have called the fraternal association of the English-speaking peoples. This means a special relationship between the British Commonwealth and Empire and the United States. This is no time for generalities, and I will venture to be precise. Fraternal association requires not only the growing friendship and mutual understanding between our two vast but kindred systems of society, but the continuance of the intimate relationship between our military advisers, leading to common study of potential dangers, the similarity of weapons and manuals of instructions, and to the interchange of officers and cadets at technical colleges. It should carry with it the continuance of the present facilities for mutual security by the joint use of all Naval and Air Force bases in the possession of either country all over the world. This would perhaps double the mobility of the American Navy and Air Force. It would greatly expand that of the British Empire Forces and it might well lead, if and as the world calms down, to important financial savings. Already we use together a large number of islands; more may well be entrusted to our joint care in the near future.

The United States has already a Permanent Defence Agreement with the Dominion of Canada, which is so devotedly attached to the <u>British Commonwealth and Empire</u>. This Agreement is more effective than many of those which have often been made under formal alliances. This principle should be extended to all British Commonwealths with full reciprocity. Thus, whatever happens, and thus only, shall we be secure ourselves and able to work together for the high and simple causes that are dear to us and bode no ill to any. Eventually there may come - I feel eventually there will come - the principle of common citizenship, but that we may be content to leave *to destiny, whose outstretched arm many of us can already clearly see.*

There is however an important question we must ask ourselves. Would a special relationship between the United States and the British Commonwealth be inconsistent with our over-riding loyalties to the World Organisation? I reply that, on the contrary, it is probably the only means by which that organization will achieve its full stature and strength. There are already the special United States relations with Canada which I have just mentioned, and there are the special relations between the United States and the South American Republics. We British have our twenty years Treaty of Collaboration and Mutual Assistance with Soviet Russia. I agree with Mr. Bevin, the Foreign Secretary of Great Britain, that it might well be a fifty years Treaty so far as we are concerned. We aim at nothing but mutual assistance and collaboration. The British have an alliance with Portugal unbroken since 1384, and which produced fruitful results *at critical moments in the late war. None of these clash with the general interest of a world agreement, or a world organization; on the contrary they help it. "In my father's house are many mansions." Special associations between members of the <u>United Nations</u> which have no aggressive point against any other country, which harbour no design incompatible with the Charter of the United Nations, far from being harmful, are beneficial and, as I believe, indispensable.*

I spoke earlier of the Temple of Peace. Workmen from all countries must build that temple. If two of the workmen know each other particularly well and are old friends, if their families are inter-mingled, and if they have "faith in each other's purpose, hope in each other's future and charity towards each other's shortcomings" - to quote some good words I read here the other day - why cannot they work together at the common task as friends and partners? Why cannot they share their tools and thus increase each other's working powers?

Indeed they must do so or else the temple may not be built, or, being built, it may collapse, and we shall all be proved again unteachable and have to go and try to learn again for a third time in a school of war, incomparably more rigorous than that from which we have just been released. The dark ages may return, the Stone Age may return on the gleaming wings of science, and what might now shower immeasurable material blessings upon mankind, may even bring about its total destruction. Beware, I say; time may be short. Do not let us take the course of allowing events to drift along until it is too late. If there is to be a fraternal association of the kind I have described, with all the extra strength and security which both our countries can derive from it, let us make sure that that great fact is known to the world, and that it plays its part in steadying and stabilising the foundations of peace. There is the path of wisdom. Prevention is better than cure.

A shadow has fallen upon the scenes so lately lighted by the Allied victory. Nobody knows what Soviet Russia and its Communist international organisation intends to do in the immediate future, or what are the limits, if any, to their expansive and proselytising tendencies. I have a strong admiration and regard for the valiant Russian people and for my wartime comrade, Marshal Stalin. There is deep sympathy and goodwill in Britain - and I doubt not here also - towards the peoples of all the Russias and a resolve to persevere through many differences and rebuffs in establishing lasting friendships. We understand the Russian need to be secure on her western frontiers by the removal of all possibility of German aggression. We welcome Russia to her rightful place among the leading nations of the world. We welcome her flag upon the seas. Above all, we welcome constant, frequent and growing contacts between the Russian people and our own people on both sides of the Atlantic. It is my duty however, for I am sure you would wish me to state the facts as I see them to you, to place before you certain facts about the present position in Europe.

From Stettin in the Baltic to Trieste in the Adriatic, an iron curtain has descended across the Continent. Behind that line lie all the capitals of the ancient states of Central and Eastern Europe. Warsaw, Berlin, Prague, Vienna, Budapest, Belgrade, Bucharest and Sofia, all these famous cities and the populations around them lie in what I must call the Soviet sphere, and all are subject in one form or another, not only to Soviet influence but to a very high and, in many cases, increasing measure of control from Moscow. Athens alone - Greece with its immortal glories - is free to decide its future at an election under British, American and French observation. The Russian-dominated Polish Government has been encouraged to make enormous and wrongful inroads upon Germany, and mass expulsions of millions of Germans on a scale grievous and undreamed-of are now taking place. The

Communist parties, which were very small in all these Eastern States of Europe, have been raised to pre-eminence and power far beyond their numbers and are seeking everywhere to obtain <u>totalitarian control</u>. Police governments are prevailing in nearly every case, and so far, except in Czechoslovakia, there is no true democracy.

Turkey and Persia are both profoundly alarmed and disturbed at the claims which are being made upon them and at the pressure being exerted by the Moscow Government. An attempt is being made by the Russians in Berlin to build up a quasi-Communist party in their zone of Occupied Germany by showing special favours to groups of left-wing German leaders. At the end of the fighting last June, the American and British Armies withdrew westwards, in accordance with an earlier agreement, to a depth at some points of 150 miles upon a front of nearly four hundred miles, in order to allow our Russian allies to occupy *this vast expanse of territory which the Western Democracies had conquered.*

If now the Soviet Government tries, by separate action, to build up a pro-Communist Germany in their areas, this will cause new serious difficulties in the British and American zones, and will give the defeated Germans the power of putting themselves up to auction between the Soviets and the Western Democracies. Whatever conclusions may be drawn from these facts - and facts they are - this is certainly not the Liberated Europe we fought to build up. Nor is it one which contains the essentials of permanent peace.

The safety of the world requires a new unity in Europe, from which no nation should be permanently outcast. It is from the quarrels of the strong parent races in Europe that the world wars we have witnessed, or which occurred in former times, have sprung. Twice in our own lifetime we have seen the United States, against their wishes and their traditions, against arguments, the force of which it is impossible not to comprehend, drawn by irresistible forces, into these wars in time to secure the victory of the good cause, but only after frightful slaughter and devastation had occurred. Twice the United States has had to send several millions of its young men across the Atlantic to find the war; but now war can find any nation, wherever it may dwell between dusk and dawn. Surely we should work with conscious purpose for a grand pacification of Europe, within the structure of the United Nations and in accordance with its Charter. That I feel is an open cause of policy of very great importance.

In front of the iron curtain which lies across Europe are other causes for anxiety. In Italy the Communist Party is seriously hampered by having to support the Communist-trained Marshal Tito's claims to former Italian territory at the head of the Adriatic. Nevertheless the future of Italy hangs in the balance. Again one cannot imagine a regenerated Europe without a strong France. All my public life I have worked for a strong

France and I never lost faith in her destiny, even in the darkest hours. I will not lose faith now. However, in a great number of countries, far from the Russian frontiers and throughout the world, Communist fifth columns are established and work in complete unity and absolute obedience to the directions they receive from the Communist centre. Except in the British Commonwealth and in the United States where Communism is in its infancy, the Communist parties or fifth columns constitute a growing challenge and peril to Christian civilisation. These are sombre facts for anyone to have to recite on the morrow of a victory gained by so much splendid comradeship in arms and in the cause of freedom and democracy; but we should be most unwise not to face them squarely while time remains.

The outlook is also anxious in the Far East and especially in Manchuria. The Agreement which was made at Yalta, to which I was a party, was extremely favourable to Soviet Russia, but it was made at a time when no one could say that the German war might not extend all through the summer and autumn of 1945 and when the Japanese war was expected to last for a further 18 months from the end of the German war. In this country you are all so well-informed about the Far East, and such devoted friends of China, that I do not need to expatiate on the situation there.

I have felt bound to portray the shadow which, alike in the west and in the east, falls upon the world. I was a high minister at the time of the Versailles Treaty and a close friend of Mr. Lloyd-George, who was the head of the British delegation at Versailles. I did not myself agree with many things that were done, but I have a very strong impression in my mind of that situation, and I find it painful to contrast it with that which prevails now. In those days there were high hopes and unbounded confidence that the wars were over, and that the League of Nations would become all-powerful. I do not see or feel that same confidence or even the same hopes in the haggard world at the present time.

On the other hand I repulse the idea that a new war is inevitable; still more that it is imminent. It is because I am sure that our fortunes are still in our own hands and that we hold the power to save the future, that I feel the duty to speak out now that I have the occasion and the opportunity to do so. I do not believe that Soviet Russia desires war. What they desire is the fruits of war and the indefinite expansion of their power and doctrines. But what we have to consider here to-day while time remains, is the permanent prevention of war and the establishment of conditions of freedom and democracy as rapidly as possible in all countries. Our difficulties and dangers will not be removed by closing our eyes to them. They will not be removed by mere waiting to see what happens; nor will they be removed by a policy of appeasement. What is needed is a settlement, and the longer this is delayed, the more difficult it will be and the greater our dangers will become.

From what I have seen of our Russian friends and Allies during the war, I am convinced that there is nothing they admire so much as strength, and there is nothing for which they have less respect than for weakness, especially military weakness. For that reason the old doctrine of a balance of power is unsound. We cannot afford, if we can help it, to work on narrow margins, offering temptations to a trial of strength. If the Western Democracies stand together in strict adherence to the principles of the United Nations Charter, their influence for furthering those principles will be immense and no one is likely to molest them. If however they become divided or falter in their duty and if these all-important years are allowed to slip away then indeed catastrophe may overwhelm us all.

Last time I saw it all coming and cried aloud to my own fellow-countrymen and to the world, but no one paid any attention. Up till the year 1933 or even 1935, Germany might have been saved from the awful fate which has overtaken her and we might all have been spared the miseries Hitler let loose upon mankind. There never was a war in all history easier to prevent by timely action than the one which has just desolated such great areas of the globe. It could have been prevented in my belief without the firing of a single shot, and Germany might be powerful, prosperous and honoured to-day; but no one would listen and one by one we were all sucked into the awful whirlpool. We surely must not let that happen again. This can only be achieved by reaching now, in 1946, a good understanding on all points with Russia under the general authority of the United Nations Organisation and by the maintenance of that good understanding through many peaceful years, by the world instrument, supported by the whole strength of the English-speaking world and all its connections. There is the solution which I respectfully offer to you in this Address to which I have given the title "The Sinews of Peace."

Let no man underrate the abiding power of the <u>British Empire</u> and Commonwealth. Because you see the 46 millions in our island harassed about their food supply, of which they only grow one half, even in war-time, or because we have difficulty in restarting our industries and export trade after six years of passionate war effort, do not suppose that we shall not come through these dark years of privation as we have come through the glorious years of agony, or that half a century from now, you will not see 70 or 80 millions of Britons spread about the world and united in defence of our traditions, our way of life, and of the world causes which you and we espouse. If the population of the English-speaking Commonwealths be added to that of the United States with all that such co-operation implies in the air, on the sea, all over the globe and in science and in industry, and in moral force, there will be no quivering, precarious balance of *power to offer its temptation to ambition or adventure. On the contrary, there will be an overwhelming assurance of security. If we adhere faithfully to the Charter of the United Nations and walk forward in sedate and sober strength seeking no one's land or treasure, seeking to lay no arbitrary control upon the thoughts of men; if all British moral and material forces and convictions are joined with your own in fraternal association, the high-roads of the future will be clear, not only for us but for all, not only for our time, but for a century to come.*

*   *

It had been a spellbinding speech. It had been captivating, and the language contained within very quickly spread around the world. The phrase "Iron Curtain" soon entered American vocabulary, referring to the territories governed under the umbrella of communism. Needless to say, the Soviet Union was highly offended by this speech, and complained vocally about it on an international level. Harry Truman, determined to be fair about it, offered Joseph Stalin the opportunity to come to the United States and deliver an oration of his own in defense of the policies of the Soviet Union. Stalin refused.

The speech coincided completely with Harry's thinking. Churchill was no longer in a position to guide and institute policy in the United Kingdom, but Harry had the authority of President of the United States. He was the nation's figurehead, the nation's representative. He could influence and ask for certain policies, and given his current popularity it would be easy to work with the United States Congress.

The moment came when the United Kingdom, financially struggling to recover from the ravages of World War II, announced it could no longer financially assist Greece and Turkey. Both nations had been ruined by the Axis powers; infrastructure had been destroyed during the Nazi retreat, people had been killed, and the governments had been left in ruin. With Britain ready to remove their support from these countries, they would be left alone in a no man's land between East and West, between Democracy and Communism, and they were much closer to the Soviet Union than the United States. It was obvious that those nations would be absorbed into the communist machine if no steps were taken.

Fresh off of Churchill's speech and watching the Soviet Union gobble up territory in Eurasia, Truman approached Congress with a proposal. He wanted the United States to pledge financial and military support to the nations of Greece and Turkey. He wanted the United States to do this in the hopes of containing the further spread of Communism, and to safeguard the rights of free people around the world:

Mr. President, Mr. Speaker, Members of the Congress of the United States:
The gravity of the situation which confronts the world today necessitates my appearance before a joint session of the Congress. The foreign policy and the national

security of this country are involved. One aspect of the present situation, which I present to you at this time for your consideration and decision, concerns Greece and Turkey. The United States has received from the Greek Government an urgent appeal for financial and economic assistance. Preliminary reports from the American Economic Mission now in Greece and reports from the American Ambassador in Greece corroborate the statement of the Greek Government that assistance is imperative if Greece is to survive as a free nation.

I do not believe that the American people and the Congress wish to turn a deaf ear to the appeal of the Greek Government. Greece is not a rich country. Lack of sufficient natural resources has always forced the Greek people to work hard to make both ends meet. Since 1940, this industrious, peace loving country has suffered invasion, four years of cruel enemy occupation, and bitter internal strife.

When forces of liberation entered Greece they found that the retreating Germans had destroyed virtually all the railways, roads, port facilities, communications, and merchant marine. More than a thousand villages had been burned. Eighty-five percent of the children were tubercular. Livestock, poultry, and draft animals had almost disappeared. Inflation had wiped out practically all savings. As a result of these tragic conditions, a militant minority, exploiting human want and misery, was able to create political chaos which, until now, has made economic recovery impossible.

Greece is today without funds to finance the importation of those goods which are essential to bare subsistence. Under these circumstances, the people of Greece cannot make progress in solving their problems of reconstruction. Greece is in desperate need of financial and economic assistance to enable it to resume purchases of food, clothing, fuel, and seeds. These are indispensable for the subsistence of its people and are obtainable only from abroad. Greece must have help to import the goods necessary to restore internal order and security, so essential for economic and political recovery. The Greek Government has also asked for the assistance of experienced American administrators, economists, and technicians to insure that the financial and other aid given to Greece shall be used effectively in creating a stable and self-sustaining economy and in improving its public administration.

The very existence of the Greek state is today threatened by the terrorist activities of several thousand armed men, led by Communists, who defy the government's authority at a number of points, particularly along the northern boundaries. A Commission appointed by the United Nations Security Council is at present investigating disturbed conditions in northern Greece and alleged border violations along the frontiers between Greece on the one hand and Albania, Bulgaria, and Yugoslavia on the other.

Meanwhile, the Greek Government is unable to cope with the situation. The Greek army is small and poorly equipped. It needs supplies and equipment if it is to restore authority of the government throughout Greek territory. Greece must have assistance if it is to become a self-supporting and self-respecting democracy. The United States must supply this assistance. We have already extended to Greece certain types of relief and economic aid. But these are inadequate. There is no other country to which democratic Greece can turn. No other nation is willing and able to provide the necessary support for a democratic Greek government.

The British Government, which has been helping Greece, can give no further financial or economic aid after March 31st. Great Britain finds itself under the necessity of reducing or liquidating its commitments in several parts of the world, including Greece.

We have considered how the United Nations might assist in this crisis. But the situation is an urgent one, requiring immediate action, and the United Nations and its related organizations are not in a position to extend help of the kind that is required.

It is important to note that the Greek Government has asked for our aid in utilizing effectively the financial and other assistance we may give to Greece, and in improving its public administration. It is of the utmost importance that we supervise the use of any funds made available to Greece in such a manner that each dollar spent will count toward making Greece self-supporting, and will help to build an economy in which a healthy democracy can flourish.

No government is perfect. One of the chief virtues of a democracy, however, is that its defects are always visible and under democratic processes can be pointed out and corrected. The Government of Greece is not perfect.

Nevertheless it represents eighty-five percent of the members of the Greek Parliament who were chosen in an election last year. Foreign observers, including 692 Americans, considered this election to be a fair expression of the views of the Greek people.

The Greek Government has been operating in an atmosphere of chaos and extremism. It has made mistakes. The extension of aid by this country does not mean that the United States condones everything that the Greek Government has done or will do. We have condemned in the past, and we condemn now, extremist measures of the right or the left. We have in the past advised tolerance, and we advise tolerance now.

Greek's neighbor, Turkey, also deserves our attention. The future of Turkey, as an independent and economically sound state, is clearly no less important to the freedom-loving peoples of the world than the future of Greece. The circumstances in which Turkey finds itself today are considerably different from those of Greece. Turkey has been spared the disasters that have beset Greece. And during the war, the United States and Great Britain furnished Turkey with material aid.

Nevertheless, Turkey now needs our support. Since the war, Turkey has sought additional financial assistance from Great Britain and the United States for the purpose of effecting that modernization necessary for the maintenance of its national integrity. That integrity is essential to the preservation of order in the Middle East. The British government has informed us that, owing to its own difficulties, it can no longer extend financial or economic aid to Turkey. As in the case of Greece, if Turkey is to have the assistance it needs, the United States must supply it. We are the only country able to provide that help.

I am fully aware of the broad implications involved if the United States extends assistance to Greece and Turkey, and I shall discuss these implications with you at this time. One of the primary objectives of the foreign policy of the United States is the creation of conditions in which we and other nations will be able to work out a way of life free from coercion. This was a fundamental issue in the war with Germany and Japan. Our victory was won over countries which sought to impose their will, and their way of life, upon other nations.

To ensure the peaceful development of nations, free from coercion, the United States has taken a leading part in establishing the United Nations. The United Nations is designed to make possible lasting freedom and independence for all its members. We shall not realize our objectives, however, unless we are willing to help free peoples to maintain their free institutions and their national integrity against aggressive movements that seek to impose upon them totalitarian regimes. This is no more than a frank recognition that totalitarian regimes imposed upon free peoples, by direct or indirect aggression, undermine the foundations of international peace, and hence the security of the United States.

The peoples of a number of countries of the world have recently had totalitarian regimes forced upon them against their will.

The Government of the United States has made frequent protests against coercion and intimidation in violation of the Yalta agreement in Poland, Rumania, and Bulgaria. I must also state that in a number of other countries there have been similar developments.

At the present moment in world history nearly every nation must choose between alternative ways of life. The choice is too often not a free one. One way of life is based upon the will of the majority, and is distinguished by free institutions, representative government, free elections, guarantees of individual liberty, freedom of speech and religion, and freedom from political oppression. The second way of life is based upon the will of a minority forcibly imposed upon the majority. It relies upon terror and oppression, a controlled press and radio, fixed elections, and the suppression of personal freedoms.

I believe that it must be the policy of the United States to support free peoples who are resisting attempted subjugation by armed minorities or by outside pressures.

I believe that we must assist free peoples to work out their own destinies in their own way.

I believe that our help should be primarily through economic and financial aid which is essential to economic stability and orderly political processes.

The world is not static, and the status quo is not sacred. But we cannot allow changes in the status quo in violation of the Charter of the United Nations by such methods as coercion, or by such subterfuges as political infiltration. In helping free and independent nations to maintain their freedom, the United States will be giving effect to the principles of the Charter of the United Nations.

It is necessary only to glance at a map to realize that the survival and integrity of the Greek nation are of grave importance in a much wider situation. If Greece should fall under the control of an armed minority, the effect upon its neighbor, Turkey, would be immediate and serious. Confusion and disorder might well spread throughout the entire Middle East. Moreover, the disappearance of Greece as an independent state would have a profound effect upon those countries in Europe whose peoples are struggling against great difficulties to maintain their freedoms and their independence while they repair the damages of war.

It would be an unspeakable tragedy if these countries, which have struggled so long against overwhelming odds, should lose that victory for which they sacrificed so much. Collapse of free institutions and loss of independence would be disastrous not only for them but for the world. Discouragement and possibly failure would quickly be the lot of neighboring peoples striving to maintain their freedom and independence.

Should we fail to aid Greece and Turkey in this fateful hour, the effect will be far reaching to the West as well as to the East.

We must take immediate and resolute action. I therefore ask the Congress to provide *authority for assistance to Greece and Turkey in the amount of $400,000,000 for the period ending June 30, 1948. In requesting these funds, I have taken into consideration the maximum amount of relief assistance which would be furnished to Greece out of the $350,000,000 which I recently requested that the Congress authorize for the prevention of starvation and suffering in countries devastated by the war. In addition to funds, I ask the Congress to authorize the detail of American civilian and military personnel to Greece and Turkey, at the request of those countries, to assist in the tasks of reconstruction, and for the purpose of supervising the use of such financial and material assistance as may be furnished. I recommend that authority also be provided for the instruction and training of selected Greek and Turkish personnel. Finally, I ask that the Congress provide authority which will permit the speediest and most effective use, in terms of needed commodities, supplies, and equipment, of such funds as may be authorized. If further* *funds, or further authority, should be needed for the purposes indicated in this message, I shall not hesitate to bring the situation before the Congress. On this subject the Executive and Legislative branches of the Government must work together.*

This is a serious course upon which we embark. I would not recommend it except that the alternative is much more serious. The United States contributed $341,000,000,000 toward winning World War II. This is an investment in world freedom and world peace. The assistance that I am recommending for Greece and Turkey amounts to little more than 1 tenth of 1 percent of this investment. It is only common sense that we should safeguard this investment and make sure that it was not in vain. The seeds of totalitarian regimes are nurtured by misery and want. They spread and grow in the evil soil of poverty and strife. They reach their full growth when the hope of a people for a better life has died.

We must keep that hope alive.

The free peoples of the world look to us for support in maintaining their freedoms. If we falter in our leadership, we may endanger the peace of the world. And we shall surely endanger the welfare of this nation.

Great responsibilities have been placed upon us by the swift movement of events.

I am confident that the Congress will face these responsibilities squarely.

*　　*

Truman could not have known the profound impact his speech would have upon history. He knew the immediate effect it would have. Greece and Turkey would be provided with money in the same sense that the nations of Western Europe had been. This would help those nations rebuild, and would help prevent them from giving into the spread of communism. But in his speech he had dedicated the United States to the preservation of the rights of free people the world over. He dedicated the United States to preventing the spread of totalitarian governments the world over. As he delivered the speech, he meant to confine the Soviet Union to its present borders. He could not know what the next forty years would have in store for the world. He could not envision the nuclear arms race that resulted in the constant menace of nuclear war. He could not imagine a shadow world of spy games as Eastern and Western powers attempted to gain influence in random countries. He could not imagine the tensions that would erupt as one country became communist and one country became democratic. Most importantly for his presidency, he couldn't imagine the impact his speech would have on a distant country when it was engaged in its own internal civil war, when communist forces fought democratic forces. It was a simple speech given by Truman asking for financial aid to be given to Greece and Turkey. It wound up becoming the foundation for American foreign policy for the next forty years.

Chapter 8

United Nations, NATO, and the Warsaw Pact

The United Nations is designed to make possible lasting freedom and independence for all its members.

- Harry Truman

The talks had been in the works for a while. In all honesty, they were a continuation of the talks that had begun back in 1918 when Woodrow Wilson was campaigning for an international organization called the League of Nations. He had been somewhat successful; a League of Nations was created, but the United States had failed to join. Despite his best efforts, Wilson could not convince the United States Senate to ratify the Treaty of Versailles. Joining the League of Nations, they had argued, could potentially force the United States to become embroiled in another global conflict. It would be best to remain neutral. After all, that's the wisdom George Washington had imparted as he left office.

But becoming embroiled in another global conflict is exactly what had happened to the United States, League of Nations or no. Without the United States, the architect nation of the organization, the League had lacked the strength and teeth necessary to deal with international threats. Hitler had capitalized on the League's reluctance to act, and had annexed Czechoslovakia and Austria before war even began. Japan had been hit by several embargoes after its invasion of China, but it was able to take the resources from China that it wasn't receiving from Europe. The League was weak and ineffective. It needed to be strengthened, and it needed the United States.

A newer, stronger organization had been discussed among the Allied Powers. Now, with the war almost over, it was time to take the necessary steps. This time Congress had not opposed the United States' entry into the organization. It hadn't hurt that the proposed headquarters would be in New York City, offering the United States front row seats in the theater of international politics. Harry was excited by the prospect, and had already been invested with that authority by the Congress. Once the United States joined, it would simply be a matter of waiting for the other nations to join before an organization for lasting peace could be created.

On August 8, 1945, Harry Truman signed the United Nations Charter, officially ratifying United States' entry into the global organization. He did it with very little fanfare, using a cheap desk pen as opposed to a ceremonial pen to sign the document. The world was not watching him sign the piece of paper. The world was captivated by reports and footage from Japan, where the two atomic bombs had been detonated on Hiroshima and Nagasaki.

It would take many more months of ceremony and signatures as World War Two drew to a close and nations began recovering from the destruction to focus on the next step. Finally, on October 24, 1945, the United Nations came into existence. Its purpose, just like that of the League of Nations, was to exist as a place where nations could come to discuss their concerns and grievances before an open forum, and find global support or condemnation. Its function was to allow nations to discuss their problems vocally, rather than resort to military force to deal with their issues. The United Nations also realized that not all problems could be solved verbally, and knew that at times it might be called on to go to war. This was a pledge not entered into lightly by the member states that joined. They were essentially entering into an alliance with every nation that joined the organization, regardless of past disagreements and disputes.

What made this situation so unique was that the five Allied Powers from World War II would become permanent members on the United Nation's Security Council. Other nations would be elected to serve for a set period of time, but the United States, United Kingdom, France, China, and Soviet Union—later Russia—would all have representatives permanently on the Council. Even as the United Nations formed, tensions between the United States and the Soviet Union were already escalating. This in turn would lead to some heated debates within the confines of the United Nations.

The five permanent member states on the United Nations have veto power. Therefore, any resolution passed by a majority of the council can be overruled by one nation state. The Cold War had intensified following Harry Truman's Doctrine wherein he outlined the risk inherent in the spread of communism, and then later when the Soviet Union successfully tested its first atomic bomb. Both nations were trying to find a distinct advantage over the other one, and both were testing their limits overseas. Most of the first decisions faced by the United Nations Security Council were vetoed by one nation or the other as it struggled to find an edge over its ideological enemy. As a result, the United Nations was slightly hamstrung in light of the escalating tension of the Cold War. Many critics argued—and still do—that the five permanent member nations had been given excessive power when it came to the right to veto. Their counter argument was that they had earned that right by winning the Second World War. If it wasn't their divine right as part of getting rid of Hitler, it was the right of the conquerors to do as they please.

The first major crisis faced by the United Nations would occur in 1949, when Korea began experiencing a civil war. China had already undergone a civil war which resulted in Communist control of that nation. Now, Korea was poised to fall to communism as well. To Truman, the threat was obvious. First one nation would fall to communism, and then another would, as if they were dominoes stacked up one beside the other. After losing China, the United States and the western world could not let Korea become communist. They approached the United Nations.

What followed was a heated debate among the member nations. They argued about the necessity of becoming involved with a sovereign nation's internal struggle, they argued over a nation's right to self-determination. Finally, when the time came for a decision, the United Nation's Security Council met to cast a vote. At the time, Communist China was not represented in the United Nations; it was still represented on the United Nations Security Council by the Democratic Chinese government currently in exile. As such, they voted along the same lines as the western powers about stopping the war in Korea. The Soviet Union, by contrast, hoped to embarrass the United Nations and invalidate the Security Council decision by boycotting the vote. Unfortunately, the terms of the United Nations were different than the terms of the League of Nations. Abstaining from a vote would not invalidate it, nor would missing a vote. By removing themselves from the table, the Soviet Union took away the only means of keeping the United Nations out of the

Communist instigated Korean War, which will be discussed in more detail in the following chapter.

Two other organizations were created soon after the end of World War II to deal with the crisis of politics. The United States and its allies would form the North Atlantic Treaty organization, or NATO, to be ready to stop the Eastern European Hegemony the Soviet Union was attempting to create. In response to the establishment of NATO, the Soviet Union created its own alliance, composed of its group of soviet satellite nations, and called it the Warsaw Pact. All the steps that were necessary for war were being taken: alliances were being created, and joint operations were conducted by the nations on both sides.

Chapter 9

Harry Truman and the Korean War

"I fired MacArthur because he wouldn't respect the authority of the president.
I didn't fire him because he was a dumb son of a bitch,
although he was."

-Harry Truman

When he had fought in World War I, it had been called the Great War, the War to end all wars. That prediction had been put to rest twenty years later when a larger conflict erupted. World War II, with its incomparable scale and violence, had taken the title. It had ushered in the atomic age; it had demonstrated how quickly an entire city of people could be extinguished from the face of the earth. Surely it would be the war to end all wars; what sane person would risk war when the result could be the end of life on earth? Yet here it was, not even ten years distant, and war once more raged.

Granted, the scope of the conflict was much smaller than World War II, confined as it was to a tiny Southeast Asian peninsula. Despite its size, however, it represented a much more tangible threat. China had already undergone a Communist revolution. The largest market in Asia had been closed to the United States. Now, as the tentacles of communism worked their way into Korea, it was becoming clear how much of a threat it was.

There seemed to be a distinct pattern emerging as one nation after another fell to communism. Proximity seemed to be the largest factor, allowing for the free flow of ideas. It was called the Domino Theory, and the theory was becoming an established fact as Communist North Koreans invaded Democratic South Korea in a vicious civil war to establish "legitimate" government. It was the first major test that would face the United Nations. Harry just hoped that the gathered nations would see the threat facing the world, and would make the right decision.

The Korean War would be the largest crucible faced by Harry Truman during his presidency. In the annals of history, Truman is remembered for two things. He ordered the dropping of the atomic bombs, and he committed the United States to war in Korea in response to the United Nation's resolution to do so. As such, this conflict will be covered in depth in this text as it is the hallmark of Truman's presidency.

The crisis in Korea was the first large scale incident that the United Nations would have a hand in. As the Communist forces of North Korea invaded the South, Harry Truman made his fears known to the assembled nations. To the United States and Harry Truman, the invasion of South Korea by the North was similar to Adolf Hitler's annexations of Czechoslovakia and Austria before World War II. He could not stand by and let it happen again, nor could the United States. The United States and its allies pushed for the United Nations to take action in the Asian peninsula, and prevent further attempts by the

Soviet Union to assert its hegemony in the Eastern Hemisphere. This resulted in an outraged Soviet Union, who vocalized their opinions loudly in the assembly of the United Nations, and in the press.

The Soviet Union, as a permanent member on the United Nations Security Council, had the opportunity to veto United Nation's involvement in Korea. Unfortunately for the Soviet Union, they attempted to make a scene of the proceedings by boycotting the meeting and not casting a vote. They assumed that the United Nations functioned just like the League of Nations, and that by abstaining from their vote, the vote of the Security Council would be invalidated. They also thought it would make the United States and its allies look like war mongers. As a result, it came as quite a shock to the communist nation when the United Nations passed a resolution to become involved in the Korean Conflict.

The United Nations passed Resolution 82, calling on all member nations to provide military assistance to the United Nations to deal with the threat posed by North Korea. On receiving consent from the United Nations to act, Truman next turned to the American Congress and asked for them to appropriate funding for the conflict, and to give Congressional approval of this support. Because it was a United Nations resolution, and not an act by the American government, the action in Korea did not require a declaration of war by Congress.

The United States Congress approved funding for the war, as well as the call for United States troops to be deployed. Due to his familiarity with the Pacific following his generalship during World War II, General Douglas MacArthur was given Supreme Allied Command of the United Nations forces deployed in Korea. Because the action was an act of defense and not of attack, MacArthur was given very clear instructions at the outset of the campaign to maintain the present separation of North and South Korea at the 38th degree of latitude. His goal was to limit the incursion of the North Koreans and contain the spread of communism. It was not to destroy the North Koreans.

As the conflict began, Truman wanted to begin operations against the North Koreans as soon as possible. He initially ordered a naval blockade of the North Korean coastline, but his order could not be carried out. He was told that the United States no longer had the naval strength to enforce such a blockade. Truman was shocked by this news, but he was also the reason for it.

Following World War II, the United States had no longer needed to spend such massive amounts of money to keep the nation on a wartime footing. Truman had ordered dramatic cuts to defense spending. The result was a much weaker army than the United States had fielded during the Second World War. In addition to that, most of the military spending had been put into building nuclear bombs. From the outset, Truman knew he would not use nuclear weapons in Korea; the Soviet Union knew this as well.

American forces began arriving in Korea from their occupation bases within Japan. Rather than waiting to build up a mass of troops, Truman and MacArthur agreed on sending small groups of American soldiers to reinforce the South Koreans. These American forces arrived in advance of the United States' Eighth Army.

The American forces first engaged the North Koreans at the Battle of Osan. 540 men of the American 24th division clashed with the Korean People's Army in an uneven match up. The American forces hadn't brought enough equipment to attack the enemy's armored vehicles. As a result, the men of the advanced element were repulsed, and the Korean People's Army pushed the American army back to Pusan.

Along this march, the Korean People's Army committed several atrocities. In an effort to destroy the intelligence services of the South Koreans and the Allied forces, the Korean People's Army killed many civil servants and intellectually inclined civilians. On hearing about these murders, General MacArthur sent a sternly worded communication to the North Korean Leader Kim Il-sung telling him that he was responsible. Kim Il-sung scoffed at the letter; after his army had driven back the Americans, he was convinced the war would be over within a month.

Kim Il-sung could confidently make this assertion because he had the support of China, and China in turn was being supported by the Soviet Union. Given their recent victory over the Americans, and the fact that the United States and United Nations forces were trapped in Pusan, it seemed the North Koreans had the advantage; but the United States had the advantage of its air force.

In an effort to break out of Pusan, the United States Air Force began a bombing campaign designed to attack North Korean supply routes and logistics. Every day they would run over forty bombing runs, bombing train tracks and roads. Although the war was being fought to stop the invasion of the communist forces, Harry Truman, as Commander in Chief, had given his troops permission to attack North Korea when it seemed necessary and practicable. As a result, the United States Air Force ran bombing campaigns into North Korea. During one of these attacks, an American bomber crew dropped bombs on a target that was actually in Chinese territory.

China was outraged by the event, but the government of China was not officially recognized in the United Nations; China was represented by the government in hiding on the island of Taiwan. In order to make the Chinese complaints heard by the United Nations, the Soviet Union brought the news to the attention of the organization, and demanded action from the United Nations Security Council. Harry Truman was hiding nothing, however, and he stepped forward following the attack. He proposed that a neutral committee of nations, including India and Sweden, should look at the incident and determine what penalty the United States should pay in compensation. The Soviet Union rejected this proposal, and its attempt to discredit the United States on the world scene failed.

As the beleaguered Americans kept up their defense of the Pusan Perimeter, they were continuously supplied with fresh troops and weapons from Japan. The United Nations military build-up in Pusan continued despite the repeated attacks of the North Koreans. Finally, by the time September rolled around, the United Nations forces outnumbered the North Korean forces 180,000 to 100,000. Following the United States Air Force bombing campaign, the United Nations forces broke out of Pusan, fighting back against the North Koreans and pushing them northward.

The North Korean army had maintained their state of war for a lengthy period of time. The soldiers were tired and their stockpiles had grown small. They also lacked the navy and the air force that the United Nations possessed. The Allies had seen this and wanted to exploit the advantage they currently possessed. General Douglas MacArthur, since the outset of the war, had proposed an amphibious landing at Inchon. Though his proposal had first been vetoed by the Joint Chiefs at the Pentagon, Truman gave him the go ahead after the break out from the Pusan perimeter.

MacArthur organized a joint task force composed of United States Army and Marines, as well as South Korean soldiers. In all, he assembled nearly 50,000 men for the attack. On the 15th of September, bombing sorties and artillery fire ripped into the defenses around the city of Inchon. Though the battle was a relatively small one, the assault destroyed most of the city. The United States Army had captured Inchon; it would be used as a stepping stone to advancing on Seoul.

Despite the fact that that Soviet Union was not going to engage itself in the conflict, Joseph Stalin, the premier of the Soviet Union, told Kim Il-sung that he would have to redeploy his army in order to protect the captured capital of South Korea. Zhou Enlai, the premier of China, told the North Koreans to hold onto

Inchon if they had at least 100,000 men; if they did not, he told Kim Il-sung that it would be wise to withdraw.

In conjunction with air raids by the United States Air Force, the soldiers of the South Korean Army were able to recapture their capital. The North Korean Army suffered heavy losses, especially of its tanks and artillery, as they were slow and cumbersome as well as exposed from the air. The battle plan of the North Koreans was thrown into disarray, as was the organization of its army. As the South Koreans recaptured Seoul and the Americans continued their aerial attacks, the North Korean army splintered and retreated. Rather than withdraw back into North Korea to protect their capital, they scattered into the wind.

By September 29th, MacArthur had restored the official government of South Korea. He also received a secret communique from the United States Defense Secretary George Marshall. The letter said "We want you to feel unhampered tactically and strategically to proceed north of the 38th parallel." Though his instructions at the outset of the conflict had been to maintain the separation between North and South Korea, he had also been advised by Truman that he could operate within North Korea to help bring an end to the war. MacArthur began planning an attack into North Korea.

China caught wind of this, and warned the United States that China was prepared to become involved in the conflict if the United States crossed the 38th parallel. The government of North Korea was being advised by China on strategies that could be used to prevent United Nations encirclement and bring about their eventual defeat.

On October 1st, the coalition of United Nations forces managed to push the soldiers of the Korean People's Army north past the 38th parallel. At that point, the soldiers of North Korea pursued the retreating forces while the remaining United Nations forces stopped at the line. They did not have the authority to move forward, and Truman would not undermine the legitimacy of the new and fragile organization. He would follow the international rule of law before he gave his commander orders to advance.

It took six days for the United Nations to authorize its combined military forces to advance past the 38th. After landing their forces and supplies at Wonsan and Riwon, the United Nations moved on to the North Korean capital of Pyongyang. The United States' 187th Airborne Regimental Combat Team made jumps into the surrounding countryside in an effort to cut off roads leading to the city and rescue American prisoners of war. Before long, the United Nations had captured over 135,000 North Korean soldiers, and put the army of North Korea on the run.

General MacArthur had crushed the back of the North Korean army. Seeing the enemy in flight, he knew he would have to destroy them before they had an opportunity to regroup and counterattack. He knew that, in order for the

United Nations to succeed, the war would have to reach into China to destroy the depots and factories supplying the North Koreans. He sent his appeal to Harry Truman, his Commander in Chief. When Truman received the request to attack into China, Truman disagreed. Instead, he told MacArthur to defend the border.

The United States had already become somewhat involved with China during the Korean War. Truman had ordered the United States Seventh Fleet into position at the Taiwan Strait in an effort to protect the Nationalist Republic of China (Taiwan) from the People's Republic of China (China). China had already prepared an invasion force for Taiwan; once it saw the United States' presence in the Taiwan Strait, Mao Zedong canceled his planned invasion of the island. He reorganized his army into the People's Liberation Army, and told his government that he would use his soldiers to intervene in Korea. China justified this position to the world by stating that it was reacting to

"American aggression in the guise of the United Nations."

The Chinese leader informed the United Nations that, because Korea was China's neighbor, it was only natural that China would be concerned about what happened in Korea. China was very worried about the solution to the "Korean Question," and informed the United Nations that in an effort to protect their national security, China would defend itself against the United Nations forces in Korea. When Truman heard this, he became infuriated, and said that it was nothing more than "a bald attempt to blackmail the United Nations." Truman dismissed these threats, not understanding how serious they were.

Following a series of talks between North Korea and China and the Soviet Union, China decided to commit to the defense of North Korea. Chinese forces began moving to the front. They marched during the night, and they set up camp during the day beneath heavy camouflage. It made them difficult to spot, which in turn meant that the United Nations' army was unprepared for China to join the offensive.

Meanwhile, President Truman and General MacArthur had been discussing the next phase of battle planning. MacArthur didn't believe that there was a significant chance of Chinese intervention, despite the letters being sent by the Chinese government. He reasoned that the Chinese only had around 400,000 soldiers they could commit, and that given the present situation of the United Nations, any such action by the Chinese would result in a slaughter. This was because the United Nations had clear air superiority, experience, and a defensive position. They were not only butting heads over what policy to pursue in Korea, but also butting heads on a personal level. The President had asked MacArthur to return to the United States to meet with him; MacArthur had refused the offer of his commander, and Truman had acquiesced and met him on Wake Island in the Pacific. It was unprecedented, and very widely publicized.

Despite MacArthur's assurances that the Chinese would not attack, the Chinese attacked the United Nations' forces on October 25th. Because they had assembled in secret, crossing great stretches of territory, the allied forces were caught unprepared. They mounted a stiff resistance, but ultimately were forced to halt their advance into North Korea and withdraw back to the Ch'ongch'on River. Following the attack, the Chinese broke off the attack and withdrew to the mountain hideouts rather than press the attack.

Despite the setback, many within the United Nations Command Team did not believe the Chinese had become involved, given their sudden withdrawal following the battle. The United States 8th Army had devised a new strategy, called the "Home By Christmas Offensive." The Eighth Army would move up the northwestern corridor of North Korea, and the United States X Corps would advance along the eastern coast. As they set out, military intelligence had failed to note the movement of the Chinese forces; the men of the United States military did not realize they were marching into a trap.

The Chinese launched their Second Phase Offensive, attacking the United Nations forces along their defensive line at the Ch'ongch'on River. The attack came in an overwhelming wave, first knocking out the Republic of Korea's II Corps, and then the 2nd Infantry Division of the United States Army. Following this attack, the decision was made to withdraw, and the United Nations Command pulled back. On the eastern front, the People's Volunteer Army of China attacked the United States' 7th Infantry Division. Caught off guard like their counterparts to the west, the 7th Infantry Division was able to withdraw under cover of an Air Force bombardment and supporting fire from the United States X Corps.

This combined offensive by Chinese forces managed to drive the soldiers of the United Nations back below the 38th by the end of November, except for a foothold in Hungnam controlled by the United States X Corps. Eventually they would have to relinquish this foothold in North Korea, in order to support the badly weakened United States Eighth Army in the south. Not only had it lost several thousand men in the attacks launched by China, but General Walton Walker, commander of the United States Eighth Army, was killed in an automobile accident. Morale had bottomed out at the end of 1950.

Walker was replaced by General Matthew Ridgway, who assumed command of the army just in time for the next phase of the Chinese offensive. On New Year's Eve of 1950, the Chinese launched the Chinese New Year's Offensive, attacking during the night to the accompaniment of loud trumpets and gongs intended to confuse the enemy. The soldiers of the United Nations were unfamiliar with this form of psychological warfare, and found it to be mentally disorienting. Many panicked and withdrew to the south. By January 4, 1951, the Chinese had helped the North Korean Army recapture the South Korean capital for the second time.

As the forces of the United Nations were overwhelmed time and again, General MacArthur contemplated the use of nuclear weapons against Chinese and North Korean targets. He intended to use not only the devastating effect of the blast, but also the radiation that was created by the bombs. He wanted the nuclear fallout to disrupt Chinese and North Korean logistics routes. Truman would not hear of it, however, and refused the General's request.

Following his appointment as Commander of the United States Eighth Army, General Ridgway began a new string of offensives. He was a charismatic leader who boosted the morale of his soldiers. In order to determine what they were up against, he committed a large block of soldiers to reconnoiter in force. This became known as Operation Roundup. Having resupplied the United States X Corps to full strength, Ridgway ordered them forward. Taking advantage of the United Nations' air superiority, Operation Roundup moved forward and eventually recaptured the Han River and the city of Wonju. After this, attempts were made through the United Nations to reach a cease-fire agreement. These negotiations failed, however, and as a result the United Nations passed Resolution 498 naming the People's Republic of China as an aggressor in the Korean War.

In response to the renewed attacks of the United Nations, the Chinese Army retaliated with their Fourth Phase Offensive, pushing back around Hoengseong. Initially, United Nations forced were pushed back, but the impetus of the Chinese attack was soon blunted by the United States 2nd Infantry Division and the French Battalion. The 5,600 soldiers of the United Nations force were overwhelmed by the 25,000 soldiers of the Chinese Army, but rather than run they stood their ground. Through their tenacious defense and air support, the soldiers of the

United Nations were able to push back the soldiers of the Chinese Army.

Following the success of Operation Roundup, General Ridgway next ordered the revitalized United States Eighth Army to advance forward. The advance would take place along the entire battlefront, and take advantage of the superiority of Allied firepower. The goal of Operation Killer was simple: kill as many North Korean and Chinese soldiers as possible. Before long, the allied army was able to recapture Seoul from the North Koreans once again. It was the fourth time in a year that the city had been conquered by friend or foe, and it now lay in ruins. The population of the city had once stood at 1.5 million people. Now, only 200,000 remained, and those who did were struggling through starvation and privations to survive amid the wreckage of their home.

In response to these offensives, China became more openly involved in the war. It boosted its wartime manufacture of munitions and weapons, it practiced large scale air defense trainings, and it began to commit the Chinese Air Force to the war in an effort to put an end to the air superiority of the United Nations.

Meanwhile, on the Allied front, big changes were making their way down the pipeline. The constant clashes between Commander in Chief and soldier had reached a breaking point, and on the 11th of April Truman removed Douglas MacArthur from the position of Supreme Allied Commander. There were several reasons for Truman's decision. MacArthur had crossed the 38th parallel, bringing China into the war and resulting in several thousand allied deaths. MacArthur had argued that it should be on his authority, and not the president's, to use nuclear weapons. MacArthur believed that the only way to achieve peace would be the complete and unconditional surrender of the North Korean forces, laughing at Truman's believe that a ceasefire and a truce could prove to be an honorable outcome. Most important was his flippant disregard for his president, and his overall lack of respect for

Truman. MacArthur was also widely criticized for never spending a night in Korea, and instead directing the war from Japan. All of these things combined led to MacArthur's dismissal. He would later be the subject of a Congressional hearing, where it would be determined that he had violated the United States Constitution by defying the orders of the President of the United States. MacArthur would be replaced as Supreme Allied Commander by General Matthew Ridgway, who had already demonstrated his capacity to lead.

Ridgway reacted promptly to the promotion and continued pushing his men forward, back to the hotly contested 38th parallel. Attacks by the United Nations continued to weaken the forces of North Korea and China, and many attempts were made by United States Paratroopers to drop behind enemy lines and trap them from their northern escape routes. In response to this increased military pressure, the Chinese acted with their Fifth Phase Offensive. The Chinese attempted to push the American forces back, first at the Battle of the Imjin River and the Battle of Kapyong. They threw over 700,000 men against the allied forces. At first they were slightly pushed back, but the United Nations' forces managed to hold the line north of Seoul and prevent the city from falling for the fifth time.

The Chinese next attacked along the Soyang River. The weight of their numbers enabled them initially to overwhelm the South Korean forces and the United States X Corps, but their attack was stopped by May 20th. The United States Eighth Army then moved into place and counterattacked, driving the North Koreans and the Chinese back to "Line Kansas," which was north of the 38th parallel.

This last counterattack by the United States Eighth Army would be the last major ground offensive of the Korean War. The United Nations Command force and the Chinese forces of the People's Volunteer Army continued to exchange fire, but neither side gained territory. The war had entered a point of stalemate, and cease-fire talks in the United Nations resumed where once they had failed.

These talks continued while Chinese and North Korean armies continued to challenge the United Nations. The renewed goal of the United Nations was to maintain the security of everything south of the 38th parallel, without seeking to expand their controlled territory. The United Nations continued a campaign of aerial bombing, severely hampering the logistics of the Chinese and North Korean armies. Eventually the casualties suffered by the Chinese forces became so great that Zhou Enlai called a conference to address the issue. He demanded increased construction of railways, and increased availability of shipping, but none of these measures addressed the issue of protecting them. Peng Dehuai, the commander of the People's Volunteer Army, told the military commission that none of the measures mentioned would alleviate the problems of the Chinese Army. The men were dying from starvation, and the Chinese had no way to counter the Allied air forces. After his outburst, the conference was brought to an end.

The armistice talks would continue for over two years. One of the biggest topics under discussion was the repatriation of prisoners of war. The problem was that many of the Chinese and North Korean soldiers did not want to be sent home to their respective countries, which the Chinese and North Korean governments found to be unacceptable.

Throughout these entire proceedings, Harry Truman was heavily involved. The Korean War had been his responsibility, it had occurred at his urging, and it had been conducted largely on his orders as Commander in Chief. He had borne the brunt of these weighty decisions, opting not to use nuclear weapons although they were available to him. He chose not to pursue a war into North Korea or China, knowing the ramification could be the third global conflict in a century. Unfortunately for Truman, it would not be on his watch that peace would be concluded.

He had decided not to run for re-election. The United States Congress had passed the twenty second amendment in 1947, limiting presidents to two terms in office. Even though this wouldn't apply to him due to his assumption of the office on the death of the president, Truman had grown weary of the office. His successor, Dwight D. Eisenhower, travelled to Korea following his inauguration to see what could be done to bring an end to the Korean War.

What was proposed was India's Korean War Armistice. The armistice created a complete cessation of all hostilities in Korea by all armed forces. This cessation of hostilities was to be enforced by the commanders of both sides of the conflict. Although this caused the fighting to stop on both sides, no agreement was made between the combatant nations; as such, the Korean War is technically still active.

The armistice also created the Korean Demilitarized Zone, known as the DMZ. This border is a 2.5 mile strip of land between North and South Korea, established along "Line Kansas," the last point of contact where the two opposing sides confronted one another. Today, the DMZ is the most heavily defended national border in the world.

Lastly, the issue of prisoners of war was discussed. It was ultimately decided that "Within 60 days...each side shall...directly repatriate and hand over in groups all those prisoners of war in its custody who insist on repatriation to the side to which they belonged at the time of capture." Over 22,000 North Korean and Chinese Soldiers refused to be repatriated, and settled within South Korea or sought asylum in the United States. Conversely, 327 South Korean Soldiers, 21 American Soldiers, and 1 British soldier declined their repatriation, and settled in North Korea or China.

The armistice brought the war to an end, although the war never officially ended in the absence of an international treaty. It had been a large conflict, with a relatively obscure ending. It had been the first battle fought under the auspices of the Truman Doctrine, the first battle testing American resolve to stem the spread of Communism. It would not be the last. The Korean War was fought to a stalemate; the result was the creation of an enemy to the United States that exists to this day, a nation still angry with the United States for its involvement in the Korean War

*   *

As has been related, the struggle was a convoluted one. Although the primary objective was to contain the spread of communism, the fear on both sides was of antagonizing the other into doing something too rash. MacArthur pushed too hard, threatening to invade China, which could have led the Soviet Union to counterattack. China, although it committed troops, was very quiet about sending them, for fear of escalating the conflict and inciting a harsher American action. The war was fought back and forth, with both sides losing tens of thousands of young men. At the end, the armistice created the Demilitarized Zone nearly exactly where the war had begun. The Korean War was largely a stalemate, due to the limited actions the commanding officers could take, as well as the uncertain ripples that a splash in that geopolitical stew could cause. The ceasefire was signed, but a formal treaty recognizing the war's end was never ratified. As the world moves into its sixty third year since the end of the conflict, the United States still exists and operates in a state of war mentality with North Korea, as the North Koreans do with the United States.

Chapter 10

Legacy on American Politics

"Men make history and not the other way around.
In periods where there is no leadership, society stands still. Progress occurs when courageous, skillful leaders seize the opportunity to change things for the better." – Harry Truman

Harry sat at his breakfast table, eating a bowl of oatmeal while reviewing the CIA daily brief. It was one of the last vestiges of office remaining to him, that and his secret service detail. He was still consulted from time to time by sitting presidents, and he enjoyed playing the role of official advisor. The job was one that never really left you; you could take the man out of the White House, but you couldn't take the White House out of the man. As he read through the briefing, nothing seemed optimistic other than the fact that the United States' stockpile of nuclear warheads exceeded that of the Soviet Union.

The Space Race had been the latest contest between the two struggling superpowers. It had begun in 1957 with the Soviet launch of Sputnik, the first artificial, man-made satellite. Under the leadership of Dwight D. Eisenhower, the National Aeronautics and Space Agency (NASA) was created to deal with the fact that the United States had fallen behind. But it had been President Kennedy, the young man who had tragically been assassinated two years previously, who had committed the immense resources of the United States to the goal of being the first nation to land a man on the moon. It was 1968, and the end of the decade was right around the corner. Not only was this deadline looming, but the United States' attention was focused elsewhere.

Around the world, in French Indochina, a conflict was raging. It had begun under Kennedy, but his assassination had shifted responsibility to Lyndon B. Johnson. As tensions escalated and the United States found itself embroiled in a protracted conflict, Johnson had famously said that he would not be the first American President to lose a war. Truman could understand his resolve, as well as the tough situation with which he was dealing. He had experienced his share of public outcry and outrage; it was the nature of the job. When he had received his lowest public approval ratings, Harry had commented that his administration would be "cussed and discussed for years to come."

His eyes read over Soviet troop movements. He scanned the briefings regarding new technologies being researched. He read about classified operations that would never see the light of day. He read the updated strength comparisons between the Warsaw Pact and NATO. His entire briefing dealt with the current conflict gripping the world. It was not confined to a war waging in Southeast Asia, nor a race to space. Those were all small subsets of a much more global conflict, one taking place on a grander scale even than World War II.

He sighed and put the papers down. The Cold War had been raging since he was president, beginning at exactly the same moment that the Second World War had ended. The world had been divided between capitalism and communism, between democratic governments and totalitarian dictatorships. It represented a struggle between good and evil on par with World War II; the future of the free world depended on its outcome. The non-violent conflict had already lasted over twenty years; based on the information in the briefings, it showed no sign of slowing down anytime.

The Cold War weighed heavily on Truman's shoulders. It had been under his leadership that it had begun. It had been his words that laid the groundwork for all future foreign policy decisions made by the American government. When he read through the CIA briefing, he was reading the consequences of his.

Truman's speech pledging American support to Turkey and Greece was the first in a series of policies that would promote American ideals at home and abroad. The speech had been made in the defense of democratic ideals and free market, capitalistic societies. He had been defending the notion that government was best which governed least, principles set in stone by Thomas Jefferson when he had written the Declaration of Independence and by James Madison when he had written the Constitution. They were words that had been meant to pledge support to the free people of those nations, offering financial assistance to their governments to prevent them from collapsing into anarchy or Communism. Eventually, they would be used by United States policy makers and be applied to the free peoples around the world. The United States had been a beacon of freedom, a bright light inviting people from across the world to come and embrace their natural rights. Beginning under Truman's presidency, the United States would break its traditional role as an isolationist power, and would bear the torch of freedom in the face of totalitarian oppression.

The Korean War had been the first extension of the policy of containment. It had been fought while Truman was in charge, and it had been fought at his discretion. The aim of the war had been limited in scope; hence the reason MacArthur had been cast aside when he became overly aggressive. The war was not being fought to eradicate communism. It was being fought to contain the spread of it, as has already been discussed. In that regard the war had been successful. The North Koreans had been stopped at the 38th parallel, exactly where the United States had become involved. It was the first war the United States had been involved in that hadn't been precipitated by an overt action against its sovereignty. Such was the nature of emerging as the "most powerful nation on earth," a distinction granted due to the fact that it was the only nation that possessed nuclear weapons. The United States could no longer afford to take a back seat. In the position of authority, it would have to deal with threats to global security, and in the eyes of most Americans, communism was the biggest threat the world faced.

Truman's speech, wherein he outlined his plans to contain the spread of communism, would have profound impacts on American foreign policy, as well as on world events. This impact would outlive his presidency as well as him. It would define over forty years of international relations. In the following sections, certain examples will be discussed to highlight the role Truman played in American politics, even after the end of his presidency.

Massive Retaliation/ Mutually Assured Destruction:

The United States of America, under the presidency of Dwight D. Eisenhower, was prepared for war. In part due to his successful career as the Supreme Allied Commander during World War II, in part because it was the nature of the daily threat the United States faced, the citizens of the United States were on a constant war footing. American civilians took shovels and bulldozers to their backyards and dug fallout shelters to prepare for nuclear winter. Children in school practiced duck and cover drills, secure in the knowledge that crouching under a wooden desk would protect them from the force of splitting atoms. The interstate system was carved across the face of America, not necessarily because it would enable the American populace to more freely move across country, but because it would enable the American military to quickly relocate from coast to coast in the event of war. In fact, by law, for every five miles of interstate highway, one mile is required to be perfectly straight in order to serve as an emergency airstrip should the need arise. America was ready for war.

Despite the preparations, decisions were being made in the higher levels of government to confront the looming threat. Dwight D. Eisenhower was tough. He was not the kind of man to let the enemy take the first swing at him, and if the enemy was able to, Eisenhower would be damned sure to fight back and beat the guy so badly that he would never represent a threat again. It was this approach to national security that led to the development of the policy of massive retaliation.

The concept was fairly straightforward. If the Soviet Union launched a nuclear missile at an American city, the United States would retaliate with all means available, including an arsenal of nuclear weapons. The idea behind the policy was to make the fear of retaliation so devastating that the Soviet Union would never take that fateful step. The other step was to make sure the Soviet Union knew about it; the threat would not serve as a deterrent if the other side didn't know it existed. Once the policy was made known, the Soviet Union replied in kind. Once this geopolitical decision had been made public, it brought the entire world to the brink of nuclear catastrophe. From 1954 until the collapse of the Soviet Communist state, this extension of the Truman Doctrine brought the world one button push away from extinction.

Bay of Pigs Invasion:

The Cold War intensified following Fidel Castro's communist takeover of Cuba in 1959. To this point, the points of contention had been Turkey and Greece, both straddling the shifting border of Democracy and Communism. For the first time, the United States was faced with a communist satellite close to its own borders. The American government began to fear the spread of communism throughout Latin America, where it had a vested interest. Following the Spanish-American War, the United States had passed the Platt Amendment; the amendment said that the United States could not annex Cuba as part of the Spanish-American War, but that it did reserve the right to intervene in Cuban affairs if Cuba began to allow itself to be influenced by foreign nations. Originally, this meant that the United States would prevent Spain from attempting to recapture the freed colony; now, over sixty years later, it would be used to prevent Soviet influence on the island.

It was John F. Kennedy's first major crisis in office, but the United States policy towards communism had been firm under Truman and Eisenhower. Kennedy met with his advisers, and then with the Central Intelligence Agency. Amongst them, an audacious People's Liberation Army was created to depose the young communist leader. When Castro had assumed power, numerous supporters of President Batista and the former democratic government had been exiled. The proposition was simple. The United States would provide military training and equipment to these expatriates, and would coordinate an assault on Cuba to help them liberate their homeland. With the funding and support of the American government, it was sure to be a success.

The Cuban exiles were trained in Guatemala by American soldiers. Finally, the day for the attack came, and they were put aboard ships. They would land their ships at the Bay of Pigs, and there storm the beaches of their homeland with guns and tanks provided by the United States. Overhead, they would receive the assistance of United States warplanes to guarantee air and ground superiority. But as the invasion crept closer, it was determined that the airplanes would demonstrate American involvement too openly. Air support for the operation was canceled.

When the Cuban exiles landed, they met with fierce resistance organized by Fidel Castro. Before long, the liberation was suppressed, and the soldiers involved in the Bay of Pigs Invasion had been rounded up. Knowing that they had been denied air support from America, they talked openly in captivity about the plan and implicated Kennedy and the Central Intelligence Agency. The Bay Of Pigs Invasion was a horribly embarrassing situation for the United States; the country had literally been caught red handed trying to overthrow another nation's government. For Fidel Castro, it was a stunning victory. Not only did he demonstrate his value to the Soviet Union, therefore receiving increased financial and military aid, but he strengthened his legitimacy in the eyes of the Cuban people. The failure of the Bay of Pigs made Castro stronger, not weaker, and made the Cuban threat to the south that much more severe.

Cuban Missile Crisis:

The next year saw tensions escalating even higher. Cuba continued to be a thorn in the heel of the Americans, perched precariously a mere ninety miles off the coast of Florida. The United States was still suffering the blow back from the Bay of Pigs invasion, and Soviet funding had been pouring into Cuba. For the Soviet Union, Cuba represented their threat to the United States. The United States had always had the distinct advantage of Turkey and Greece. Through those nations, Soviet movement through the Bosporus was limited, and when the United States developed missile sites in these countries, it gave them a decisive first strike capability over the Russians. With Cuba, the Soviet Union had turned the tables, and it began to capitalize on that.

In 1962, a United States spy plane took pictures as it flew over Cuba. When the images were printed, the story they told was horrifying. Cuba, with the help of the Soviet Union, was beginning to construct missile silos. The threat was obvious. The Soviet Union would have the ability to launch a nuclear strike at the United States well before the latter could have a chance to react. Cuba gave the Soviet Union a decisive advantage in a nuclear conflict. Fortunately for the United States, there was one element the Soviets were missing. Although the silos were nearing completion, it did not appear that any missiles had arrived. If the United States was to retain its tactical advantage, it would have to act decisively, and it would have to act quickly. And Kennedy acted.

With little regard for international law, Kennedy placed the island of Cuba under quarantine. Quarantine was a euphemism for blockade, and a blockade is an act of war. Through this edict, he forbade anything being shipped by the Soviet Union to enter into Cuban territorial waters. This decision was justified any number of ways, from citing the Monroe Doctrine to espousing the Roosevelt Corollary, then using the most recent policy of the Truman Doctrine. Regardless of the language used to coat it, it defied laws that safeguarded the freedom of the seas at the same time that it violated Cuba's national sovereignty. But with the grim specter of nuclear war hovering on the horizon, little heed was given to such trivialities.

The Russian fleet, which had set sail with the hardware necessary to complete the silos, as well as the missiles to arm the silos, barreled across the Atlantic towards the waiting line of American warships. Phones in Moscow and Washington, D.C rang off the hook as ambassadors and leaders spoke to one another, attempting to negotiate terms. But with America threatened so closely, Kennedy was not willing to budge from the line he had drawn in the sand. As the two navies neared one another, the world braced for the outbreak of the Third World War. American warplanes and Soviet warplanes, all of them armed with nuclear missiles, were scrambled and directed towards one another, missile silos opened and awaited the keyed in commands to fire. Officers in both navies had orders to fire. It was the biggest game of chicken the world had ever seen, and the consequences if no one turned would merely be the destruction of all life on earth.

Though neither leader wanted to appear weak, Kennedy had more at stake than Khrushchev. As the navies neared firing range, as the air force pilots were about to open fire, the Soviet Premier gave the order to stand down. Nikita Khrushchev had blinked, he had given the order and his fleet turned. This was the closest the world had ever, or has ever, come to thermonuclear war. It is the closest mankind has ever come to a self-inflicted extinction event on our planet, and it all happened because the policy of the United States was to contain the spread of communism.

Vietnam War:

Of all the events that occurred during the Cold War, none was more polarizing on the issue of containment than the Vietnam War. To the rest of the world, it represented just another conflict. It was nothing major or severe. The French supported the action in Vietnam because it had once been their colony, and they had just fought a twenty year war against the North Vietnamese forces before losing at the battle of Dien Bien Phu. Much like Korea, the conflict raging in Vietnam was between Northern communist forces, whose northern border stretched to Communist China, and Democratic forces in the South. When the French determined that their position was no longer tenable, they appealed to their allies in the North Atlantic Treaty Organization, and to the United Nations. The United States, fresh off the Bay of

Pigs Invasion and the Cuban Missile Crisis, could not allow another nation to fall to Communism. The impetus of the totalitarian giant was growing too large.

Under the presidency of John F. Kennedy, the United States began to send military advisers to South Vietnam. John F. Kennedy had steered the nation through two harrowing ordeals, and he had emerged triumphant from the Cuban Missile Crisis after forcing Khrushchev to back down. Then tragically, in 1963, President Kennedy was assassinated while visiting Dallas, Texas. The news stunned the American population, filling them with fear and uncertainty. Even more uncertain was the course the United States would take in Vietnam; the plan had died with the President.

Lyndon B. Johnson assumed the office, and quickly set to work enforcing the ideals contained in the Truman Doctrine. The United States would contain the spread of communism; Vietnam would be no different than Korea. Johnson committed to a massive troop buildup in Vietnam, sending over 500,000 soldiers, and then asking Congress to impose the draft. New technologies, like napalm, made the war horrific, but another innovation really shaped the course of the Vietnam War.

During World War II and the Korean War, the press had been limited. Typically, they had worked very closely with the White House. During the Vietnam War, however, a new style of reporter came out, one determined to be the first to report on events, and one determined to tell the unabridged truth. It didn't help that the United States government was still reeling from the insinuations contained in the Bay of Pigs invasion, or that politics as a whole had become determinedly secretive as the Cold War intensified. Reporters brought the news back to the home front, and the news they reported wasn't pretty and heroic.

Vietnam was a different type of war. Oftentimes the fighting occurred in dense jungle foliage, soldiers shooting at enemies they never saw. The people of Vietnam were reluctant to help American soldiers; in some cases the enemy soldiers would pose as civilians and then attack the Americans from the rear. It made the American soldiers distrustful of the Vietnamese people as a whole, and sometimes the soldiers vented their frustrations. In one classic piece of footage, a reporter is interviewing an American soldier. As the interview is taking place, and enemy soldier, his hands bound, is dragged into the middle of the street, and there is shot in the head by a United States officer. This grisly footage, when it made its way to the United States, served only to make the American people question the reason they were there.

The reason they were there was Harry S. Truman and his policy of containment. It had been the guiding focal point of American foreign policy since he first uttered those words back in the 1940's. Now, nearly 30 years later, The United States was involved in its longest, most unpopular conflict. It was a war where success was measured by body count, not by clearly distinguishable objectives. As reports of the dead and injured came in, and as Americans started to look at the events taking place, the one conclusion they came to was that they didn't need to be there. Protests began. A counter culture movement began, giving birth to the iconic hippies who flouted the authority of the American government, in one instance symbolically placing a flower into the open end of a rifle.

The war was divisive in American opinion, and it made many people distrust the American government. Worse, it made them question the ideals and concepts on which the United States was founded. America, the great beacon of freedom, was not allowing a nation half a world away to determine what kind of government it wanted. America, the home of the brave, was murdering civilians. All of this was done in an effort to contain the spread of communism; many Americans began to question whether communism truly needed to be contained to that extent.

Popularity for the war declined as the draft was imposed. Many Americans became draft dodgers, not caring to go and die in a foreign country for a cause they didn't think was worthy of it. Soldiers vocally questioned orders, or joined in the protests. Why should they have to go and die to stop a distant land from becoming communist?

The answer to this, and to all the events that spanned the era known as the Cold War, can be found in the policy developed by Harry Truman. By pledging American arms and finances to containing the spread of communism and protecting the rights of all free people, the United States became a global presence which occasionally intervened into the sovereignty of other nations. The Cold War lasted for over forty years, spanning every decade from the end of the Second World War until the symbolic moment when the Berlin Wall was torn down. Seven other United States presidents would build their foreign policy decisions around the precepts first introduced by Harry Truman in the postwar world. It created a militaristic culture in the United States, as well as around the world.

Nations of the West adopted the same containment policies as the United States. Countries like the United Kingdom and France and West Germany increased their military strength in the face of the threat from the Warsaw Pact. Each acted in their overseas territories to prevent communism from spreading. As the Western nations strengthened their position, so too did the forces of Communism. Both sides continued escalating in the face of build-up from the opposing side. Untold sums of money on both sides were committed to defense spending, NATO, and the Warsaw Pact, trying to gain the upper hand while at the same time trying to defend themselves.

Truman's speech to Congress asking for aid to Turkey and Greece had caused it all. It had placed the United States on a purposeful collision course with the Soviet Union. The United States had broken its isolationism to safeguard the free world from the spread of totalitarianism. History remembers the Mutually Assured Destruction policy of Eisenhower, or the struggles faced by Kennedy. Students learn about the military and economic pressure that Reagan placed on the Soviet Union. None of this would have happened but for Harry Truman.

Truman had understood the threat represented by the Soviet Union. Although he couldn't have imagined the Cuban Missile Crisis or the Berlin Wall, he could understand the terror that would have resulted from a world run by a totalitarian government. He knew the United States was the only force capable of stopping the communist juggernaut, and it was with determination and assuredness that he placed the nation on the path. The effects of his decision would soon spread to all western powers, and would trickle through the years into the decisions made by others. With his decision to support Greece and Turkey, Harry S. Truman had divided the world into East and West.

Epilogue

America was not built on fear. America was built on courage, on imagination, and an unbeatable determination to do the job at hand.

- Harry Truman

Harry S. Truman lived the American dream. He had grown up a poor country boy in America's bread basket. He had worked hard all of his life, not always succeeding, but never giving up. He knew, as did all Americans, that hard work and perseverance would pay off in the long run. He was a man who put family and country before himself, working hard to provide a living for his struggling family, and then volunteering to serve his country when it needed him during World War I. On his return from the war, he dedicated the remainder of his life to public service.

He rose to prominence in politics in an age where politics was a corrupt business.

Though he was supported by a man well known for his corruption, Harry kept his reputation clean and spotless. He was a man known for his honesty and integrity, he was a man known to put the people before himself, and he was a man known to work tirelessly on a project until it was completed. His political career, once begun, shot meteorically to the top. Within twenty years he occupied not only the office of Vice President, but then the office of President following the death of Franklin Roosevelt.

He had come to power at a time of transition. The world had just emerged from a global depression and a global war. New political trends were spreading across the earth, taking advantage of the power vacuum that encompassed most of the world. In characteristic Truman fashion, he dedicated the United States to uphold the virtues and values contained in the Declaration of Independence, regardless the cost. Much like himself, he wanted to commit the United States to being a nation of integrity and righteousness in the face of global uncertainty.

The decisions made by Truman while he was president had lasting effects on both the United States and the world. His policies divided the world between East and West, between communism and democracy, between good and evil. The United States would firmly uphold his policies, sometimes at the expense of peace, and sometimes with the threat of global thermonuclear war. Though he couldn't have foreseen all the paths that would open up during the Cold War, he would staunchly support the decisions of the sitting Presidents as they made decisions to combat the growing influence of the Soviet Union.

Until the end he remained a regular man, having never let power go to his head. When his term as president expired, he and his wife Bess packed up the family car and drove themselves from Missouri to the east coast, incognito. Harry didn't want to retire from the presidency and use the title to earn some lucrative job afterwards. Like his hero Cincinnatus, Truman wanted to give up power and return to the peace of his home. But he had become a celebrity, and the anonymity he sought at the end of his presidency could not be found.

He turned to other pursuits, like the construction of his Presidential library. There, he would meet in the conference room with dignitaries, biographers, and classroom students. Truman had been a bookworm growing up; his library would be one of his favorite legacies. Truman had never been a self-promoter; it's one of the reasons he tends to be overlooked in history.

Despite his relative obscurity, however, very few presidents have had such a dramatic impact on American politics. Harry S. Truman might not be as well-known as Washington, or Lincoln, or Roosevelt, but his political legacy would shape the United States in a way that very few presidents ever do. Harry Truman assumed the reins of government when the United States had become the world's greatest military and economic power. To this day, seventy years later, the United States still occupies that position, thanks entirely to Harry S. Truman.

The nation mourned as news spread that Harry S. Truman, 33rd president of the United States, had died of heart failure following complications with pneumonia. He had left the office of the presidency nearly twenty years before, but he had continued to play the role of public servant. He had been consulted by the esteemed men who had occupied his office after him, and had offered his advice and opinion on the world events taking place. He had been a small town Missouri farm boy who had become the leader of the free world. He had unintentionally created an American institution, an America that vocally and physically championed democracy overseas in the oppressive face of communism.

The ceremony was a small one. They had opted not to go through the elaborate intricacies of a state funeral and all the symbolism that went into that. Instead, Harry had decided to be buried at the Harry S. Truman Presidential Library and Museum, at Independence, Missouri. Close friends and family had been invited, and dignitaries both foreign and domestic had extended their condolences. The whole affair was a quiet thing; it would be overshadowed the following month by the elaborate funeral procession of Lyndon B. Johnson, who would die of a heart attack. For thirty days, the nation's flags would fly at half-staff for Truman.

On his tombstone, Bess had had engraved his birth date, his death date, the birthdate of his daughter Margaret, and a list of all the public offices he held, up to President of the United States. It was a fitting designation, as politics was the one thing he had exceeded triumphantly in. It was also an important gesture. Truman's life was about service: service to his family, service to his friends, and service to his country. Truman was laid to rest in the courtyard of his Presidential library, and there Bess joined him ten years later. There, both of them sleep as Americans continue to pay their respects to the man who ignited the Cold War, to the man who had divided the world.

Bibliography

About Education. "Winston Churchill's Iron Curtain Speech." Accessed March 27, 2016. http://history1900s.about.com/od/church illwinston/a/Iron-Curtain.htm

Ambrose, Stephen E. *Rise to Globalism. American Foreign Policy since 1938.* 5th rev. edn. New York: Penguin, 1988.

The Avalon Project, Yale Law School. "Truman Doctrine." Accessed March 27, 2016. http://avalon.law.yale.edu/20th_century/trudoc.asp

Gosnell, Harold F. *Truman's Crises. A Political Biography of Harry S. Truman.* Westport, Connecticut: Greenwood Press, 1980.

Harry S. Truman Library and Museum. "Harry Truman's World War I." Accessed March 17, 2016. http://www.trumanlibrary.org/whistlestop/study_collections/ww1/

McCullough, David. *Truman.* New York, New York: Simon and Schuster, 1992.

Miller Center of Public Affairs, University of Virginia. "Harry S. Truman." Accessed March 20, 2016. http://millercenter.org/president/truman.

Wikipedia. "Harry Truman." Accessed March 20, 2016. https://en.wikipedia.org/wiki/Harry_S._Truman.

Wikipedia. "Korean War." Accessed March 24, 2016. https://en.wikipedia.org/wiki/Korean_War

Printed in Great Britain
by Amazon